MONASTERY OF ST. JOHN THE THEOLOGIAN

1. *Patmos after Choiseul-Gouffier, 1782 (detail) (p. 21).*

S.A. PAPADOPOULOS
Archaeologist

MONASTERY OF ST. JOHN THE THEOLOGIAN

HISTORICAL-ARCHAEOLOGICAL GUIDE

PATMOS 1977
MONASTERY OF ST. JOHN THE THEOLOGIAN

The Brotherhood of the Monastery of St. John the Theologian on the occasion of the 20th anniversary of Greek Scholarship in Patmos, issues this new edition of the Guide and dedicates it to the founders of Patmian Studies, I. Sakkelion, I. Florides and G. Papazoglou.

The Dodecanese Islands lie in the south-eastern part of the Aegean Sea spreading between Crete, the Cyclades, and the coast of Asia Minor. Rhodes is considered to be the loveliest, Patmos the holiest of the Dodecanese Islands since it was here that St. John wrote the Revelation.

Patmos is one of the smallest of the Aegean Islands (appr. 34 square kilometres). Like most of its neighbouring isles, it is rocky and arid with scant vegetation. Its coastline presents an impressive and rich variety of beautifully formed bays, promontories and havens. Patmos has an excellent climate, a pure, transparent atmosphere, lovely vistas, crystal clear waters, sheltered harbours and, above all, golden sunshine.

Today, the population of the island is appr. 2.500 inhabitants living mainly in three areas: Chora, the medieval town built on the summit of a hill (170 metres), Scala, the port built at a later date (c. 1816), and Kambos, the rural village (see map on front cover). The small meadows lying in the interior of the bays; the tiny patches of arable land hanging on the hillsides; seasonal pasturage and fishing offer very limited possibilities of sustenance to the islanders. Hence, a large number of them move to the urban centres of Greece, emigrate to America and Australia, or go to sea.

Patmos is placed on the main tourist boat-line between Rhodes and Pireus and is, therefore, easy of access. Travelling facilities include five ships calling regularly at the island during the week, a local passenger boat, and 15 luxurious cruise boats which touch for half-day visits. Because of the clean and comfortable accomodation provided (9 hotels); the picturesque shopping centre; the warmth and hospitality of its inhabitants; its physical beauties and the holy traditions and treasures preserved in the age-old Monastery of St. John the Theologian, Patmos has become one of the most popular Greek tourist centres. This is confirmed by the fact that the number of tourists increases yearly and travelling facilities are constantly improved (for a tour of the isle see special guide: S. A. Papadopoulos, *Patmos: a visitor's guide,* Athens, 1967, and the map of Patmos).

THE HISTORY OF PATMOS

Until recently the Mediterranean was considered to be immense. Its vital centres were its closed seas — the area of action for boats and caiques — each a little world seeking communication with the other worlds. To all, the term "navigation" meant "coasting" because a coastline and islands offering safe harbour, insured provisions, which ships constantly require, gave protection against pirates and facilitated trading and orientation. Very few "navigate" as there has always been a shortage of shipbuilders, of sailors and pilots. The shores (Dalmatia, the Aegean, Syria) or, shall we better say, the **sea villages** nourishing such men, as well as the areas producing the timber necessary for ship building, are very few indeed. A basic presupposition for the existence of such villages is their proximity to a large city which supplies the special accoutrements needed by ships, the capital, the clients, the merchandise and the trading routes connecting it with the country's interior. Hence, the fate of these villagers, which is determined by the geographical position, the natural environment and the local traditions, also depends on others.

They are part of the larger fate of the Mediterranean: they flourish, decline and return again to the humble rythms of daily life which persists unaltered through the ages. History — which takes advantage of them and uses them — sooner or later takes back what it has given.

One of these sea villages is Patmos: a barren island which, even when intensely cultivated and in years of very good crop, can hardly sustain its inhabitants for two months. Therefore, its very survival would be impossible without ships and, we might add, the coast of Asia Minor lying across. For Patmos, constant points of reference are: the city of Miletus, in ancient times; of Ephessus, after the 1st century; of Anaea, during the Byzantine period (13th century); of Palatia and Smyrna during the Turkish occupation. Merchants, pirates, war fleets of Powers claiming the Aegean —all come to anchor at its excellent harbours. Abbots and skippers are obliged, passively or actively, to co-operate with everyone since the roles (soldier, pilgrim, pirate, merchant) change and symbiosis is the only choice offered for survival. The Monastery bred many leaders. Its archives often reveal their extraordinary political acumen.

It is only possible to form a very general picture of life on **Patmos in the pre-christian era** mainly because of the scant information provided by ancient authors, the restricted and as yet unexplored archeological evidence and the slim references given by travellers who visited the island during the Turkish occupation. From the Mycenean (1600-1100B.C.) and the geometrical (1100-800B.C.) periods only pottery fragments survive on the hill of Castelli (see map) which seems to have been naturally fortified. Wall remains confirm the existence of an ancient town built between the three ports of Scala, Holhaca and Mericha. Ancient cemeteries (Etia, Kambos), rock chiselling (Kalikatsou), foundation remains, architectural parts encased in the walls of christian churches, inscriptions, funerary bas-reliefs and various other discoveries inform us of the life and local cults of Patmos (Patmian Artemis, Apollo Karnios) as well as of the evolution of sculpture and of ceramic art on the island. The temple of Patmian Artemis was probably situated on the site where the Monastery stands today (inscription, architectural remains). Blessed Christodoulos "first destroyed an idol which had been erected there with great art in the name of Artemis" and then built his Monastery. The temple of Apollo was near the harbour. This important period in the history of Patmos still awaits systematic research and presentation.

However, surviving inscriptions allow us to believe that Patmos, "glorious island of Leto, daughter of Artemis", was at the end of 1st century A.D., a potent fort of Miletus, situated on its western sea boundaries (see fortifications at Castelli). Inscriptional data about temples, a gymnasium, contests and a guild of torch-bearers inform us about the island's inhabitants, their economic prosperity and cultural level. Since Patmos belonged to Miletus, the authorities must have felt trustful of the people and thus St. John the Theologian was removed thither.

The history proper of Patmos begins in the year 95 A.D. "In the beginning was..." St. John the Divine (fig. 2). "I, John, who also am your brother, and companion in tribulation, and in the kingdom and patience of Jesus Christ, was in the isle that is called Patmos, for the word of God, and for the testimony of Jesus Christ. I was in the Spirit on the Lord's day, and heard behind me a great voice, as of a trumpet, saying, I am Alpha and Omega, the first and the last: and, what thou seest, write in a book, and send it unto the seven churches..."

2. St. John the Theologian, icon (p. 56).

3. Monastery of the Apocalypse after Choiseul-Gouffier, 1782 (p. 8).

(Revelation: I, 9-11). In 95 A.D., at the time of the persecutions of the Emperor Domitian, St. John was removed "for the testimony of Jesus Christ" to the little island of Patmos. During his exile, which lasted for many months (he was recalled in 97 A.D.,) he wrote the Revelation as he himself asserts and as the old ecclesiastical writers Clement of Alexandria, Origen, Ireneus, Eusebius and others confirm. This text brought a message of hope and encouragement to the persecuted churches of Asia Minor, enriched eschatological literature with a monumental contribution and provided art with an inexhaustible source of inspiration. Patmos enters history with this text.

According to early tradition the sacred text was written in the grotto which now forms part of the lower, eastern section of the **Monastery of the Apocalypse** (fig. 3). This Monastery was built and fortified in the 17th century, while new buildings were added in the beginning of the 18th and 19th centuries. The Monastery is composed of cells, courtyards and chapels. There is one dedicated to St. Artemios and one to St. Anne (early 17th cent.) which is built in front of the cave, another to St. Nicolas (18th cent.). The **sacred cave** (fig. 4) has been transformed into a small church dedicated to St. John the Divine (the Theologian). Local tradition finds evidence of his stay here in the impressions left on the spots where he rested his head, placed his hand to raise himself up, or spread his parchment to write, as well as in the cleft on the rock from which he heard "the great voice, as of a trumpet". This tiny, dimly lit grotto became the centre of contemplation and of worship for the christian world.

An apocryphal text of a later date, which is attributed to St. John's disciple Prochoros (not mentioned in any other documents) describes in detail **St. John the Divine's sojourn in Patmos.** The text is entitled: *Travels or Miracles of St. John the Theologian, Apostle and Evangelist, set down by his disciple Prochoros* (fig. 26). The text is considered with some probability to date from the 5th century, though some scholars place it in the 4th others in the 13th century. This text is the source from which all local, oral tradition concerning St. John's stay on the island derives. It gives a detailed description of the composition of the Gospel according to St. John —a view held widely since the 11th century but not accepted today. The apocryphal text refers to various miracles performed by St. John before coming to Patmos; to his fight on the island with the magician Cynops and the fatal consequences this had for the wonder-maker idolater; to the difficulties and final success of the apostolic mission of St. John in Patmos. The islanders point to the foreign visitor the places mentioned in the narrative and the fishermen point to the petrified figure of Cynops, sunk beneath the harbour's watery floor. Monks show us the frescoes in the outer narthex which depict all these scenes (see: p.32).

Architectural parts encased today in the main church (especially the outer narthex) and in other sections of the monastery, or even in different churches in Chora and other parts of the island, confirm the fact that churches were built on the island between the 4th and 6th centuries. The most significant of these was erected on the site where the Monastery stands today. Like many other Aegean islands, we find Patmos deserted after the 7th century. This is the era of great naval battles between the Arabs and the Byzantines and of intense piratical activity undertaken by the former. The island remains deserted till the 11th century. John Kameniates who found himself accidentally in that region in the year 904 A.D., informs us: "Voyaging thus, we came to an island called Patmos, where we stayed six days, enduring most grievous trials, for the place was arid and thirst afflicted the prisoners" *(Fall of Salonica, chp. 68).* Patmos re-enters History in the end of the 11th century, when the Blessed Christodoulos founded the Monastery of St. John the Theologian.

The Blessed Christodoulos (d. March, 1093) is one of the best representatives of monastic life in this period. He was a deeply devout monk, a strict Superior, an energetic founder of monasteries, an experienced doctor, an able leader in times of war, a scholar with a passion for books (he possessed a considerable library), of humble, peasant origin yet a person of authority in the Emperor's court and in the Patriarchate, an ascetic with a profound knowledge of men and of the world, sound in his judgment and adamant in his faith — a personality, in other words, typical of the troubled age of the Comnene dynasty. He was born in a village near Nicaea of Bythinia in Asia Minor. As a hermit, he lived on mount Olympus of Myssia, in the desert of Palestine, on mount Latros near Miletus, where he was made Superior, on mount Strovilos in Caria and in the islands of Cos, Patmos and Eubea. He travelled from Rome to Jerusalem. Though a monk, he led an adventurous life tried now by the threat of the Turk, now by lay opposition, piracy or the pusillanimity of his companions.

His greatest work was the **founding of the Monastery of St. John the Theologian** (1088). "My one desire", he wrote, "was to possess this island". It was the splendour of its tradition, the sense of isolation and the fact that this island was sparsely populated that drew him irresistibly. He went to Constantinople and requested the the island be

4. Cave of the Apocalypse (p. 8).

given him that he may establish there "a workshop of virtue". His request was granted as well as the guarantee that the island would be "relieved of all obligations to the State" in exchange for his land holdings in Cos and Strovilos (he retained only those in Leros and Leipso). In the Monastery archives we can still see today the chrysobull of Alexius 1st Comnenos bestowing the island to Christodoulos and granting him the right "to be its absolute ruler in all eternity, and in such manner that no man shall ever have the power to deprive him of this priviledge". Another chrysobull grants him the free use of a private ship for the needs of the Monastery, while a third confirms exemption of the island from taxation. These chrysobulls were issued in 1088. In the Act ceding the island (August 1088) we find a description of the place which seems to have purposely exaggerated the facts: "... it is deserted, fallen to waste, covered with brambles and thorny scrub, untrodden and so arid as to be totally barren and infertile..." In his Regulation (May 8, 1091) and his secret testament (March 10, 1093) the Blessed Christodoulos gives a vivid description of the hardships he had to face during the first years of his stay in Patmos. He mentions the cowardice of his companions "... it is for this reason that Patmos is such an island, uninhabited because it has been raided and its inhabitants taken captives by the Arabs, the Corsairs, the Turks and all the others, and my monks, not having been convinced by my works, gave way to fear and refused to stay in

Patmos and departed leaving me alone..." He tells of their escape and settlement in Eubea, where he died on the 16th of March 1093 having left orders to his companions to continue his work on Patmos. His body was later brought back to the Monastery and soon became famous throughout the Mediterranean for "the miraculous cures it wrought". Greeks, Italians, Sicilians, French — all came seeking his help and often, as was the case with the Normans in 1186, tried to carry off his relic. His death anniversary is commemorated on the 16th of March and the translation of the sacred relic on the 21st of October.

The **12th century** was a century of trials. The island was poor and desolate and under the constant threat of pirates. The Turks raided the island in 1091/2; the Saracens in 1127 and 1157/8; the Normans in 1186/7; and, in short, all those who preyed the Aegean, crusaders or pilgrims, merchants or pirates, created an atmosphere of general insecurity. Visits from powerful princes often had unfortunate consequences for the island, as when Phillip-Augustus of France landed on Patmos after the third Crusade. Short term occupations resulted in heavy taxation. The oppressive intervention of Byzantine officials and neighbouring Bishops (of Icaria) who sought to subject independent Patmos to their jurisdiction render the island's survival problematical. The perseverance of Christodoulos' successors, the benefactions of the faithful, finally, imperial and patriarchal support (the Monastery is granted full autonomy in 1132 being answerable only to the Patriarchate) which is expressed through an uninterrupted extension of the old yet constantly challenged privileges, the granting of new ones — such as the shipping of settlers to the island, subsidies and grain supplies from Crete — enable the Monastery to survive this first, critical period and by the end of the 12th century to flourish. During this period, the Monastery has 150 monks, land-holdings (metochia) in Leipsos, Leros, and Crete (1195), Asia Minor, Lemnos and Chios, as well as two, tax-free ships (1197) trading freely in all ports of the Empire. The Monastery is being decorated with mural paintings (chapel of the Virgin), an extensive Library and a Treasury are formed, many members of the Brotherhood rise to the ranks of Bishop and Patriarch. The appearance of the island changes: to the north, we witness the creation of a settlement (Choridakia) where workers attached to the Monastery live with their families. The settlement is strictly out of bounds for the monks.

The **13th century,** though not without difficulties, is a century of progress: settlers arrive, the small fleet grows (4 ships after 1264), the Monastery's estate is enriched through donations, purchases and land concessions in Cos (1298), Limnos and Asia Minor. The Monastery gains in fame and authority thanks to its economical growth, its spiritual activities, the extension (partial or total) of old and the granting of new privileges, the patronage of its "Ephors" — persons, usually, of very high standing, — the miracles wrought at the saint's shrine. The creation of the town Chora around the Monastery, strengthens its defence. Yet, the incursions "of the infidel Italians and the impious pirates" continue, as well as the contestations concerning the privileges and wealth of the Monastery. The monks keep up the struggle. **Between the end of the 13th century and the beginning of the 15th,** Patmos undergoes a very difficult period, about which very little is known. Byzantine rule in the southeastern part of the Aegean weakens (end of 13th, beginning of 14th century); on the Asia Minor coast two Turkish emirates are established; the Hospitalers conquer Rhodes (1308) and all the Dodecanese islands. Patmos is placed between the boundaries of two worlds that clash. It experiences incessant, destructive incursions in times of war, piracy in times of peace. Population displacements plague the Aegean. The Monastery loses its holdings (metochia). The island survives thanks to its poverty, its insignificance and the presence of the Monastery. The information we have concerning the shipment by the monks of their settlers to Crete, is quite characteristic of the state of affairs.

The situation continues the same after the conquest of Asia Minor by the Othoman Turks (1390). The "village" of Patmos, as of the beginning of the 15th century, pays tribute to the Turk — a very small sum considering its importance (First mention of the "village", or "community" of Patmos occurs in 1454). In connection with this tribute, Buondelmondi (1406) states that the Turks not only do they not disturb the monks but provide them with all the necessaries when they cross to Asia Minor for provisions.

The clashes between the Hospitalers and the Turks (1451-81; 1491-1512) made **the 15th century** an especially hard period. Though the island is under Turkish administration since 1456 and has the right to ask for protection, it is obliged, and can do so because of its position, its relative obscurity and the continuous affrays, to seek the protection of the western powers: the Pope, the Venetians, the Hospitalers. It repays these powers by passing to them information concerning the movements of the infidel. The difficulties are such that the desertion of the island is contemplated (1500). The Monastery has 60 monks (1461) and in order ot survive these hard times it finds recourse to alms (1499, 1502, 1507). Many prelates from Asia Minor and the Aegean seek refuge at the Monastery.

During the 16th century, the occupation of the Dodecanese by the Turks (1522) as well as the end of the wars between Turks and Venetians (1540) bring some respite. The Berber pirates now move their centre of activity to the southern Mediterranean. Repopulation and cultivation of the island bring back a sense of life. The French, English, Italian and Dutch merchants, who succeed the Venetians, carry an intense and highly competitive trading activity in the ports of the Turkish Empire. The era of capitulations has began. The Turks restrict themselves to the collection of a relatively heavy tax. They do not settle on Patmos (as a rule they avoid small, poor, unfortified islands) but provide protection to the Monastery and its people on land and sea. Piri-Re'is writes (1521) that Turks and Christians alike respect and do not attack the ships of Patmos. The Hospitalers extend the right to the ships of the Monastery to travel under their own flag. The Patmiots make good use of their maritime tradition and utilize to the full the privileges that have been granted to the monastery, as well as the new political and economical conditions that have been created in the eastern Mediterranean. They continue transporting goods, cover the import needs of the island, export their famour artifacts, carry all that is needed for the Monastery from the metochia (land holdings) and tap all those resources which their poor island cannot offer.

Trade, shipping and voyaging become the main occupations of the Patmiots. Towards the end of the 16th century large, beautiful houses and numerous churches are built and a different, higher way of life appears on the island. A new social and political power is formed: the lay community of Patmos. Valuable information concerning this period is provided by the **travellers,** though it is often wrong and hardly objective. Most of these travellers never set foot on the island and based their reports on hearsay, or copied from others who were equally misinformed. Some visited the island, but only a few had the

5. *Macarios Kalogheras (p. 21).*

time or interest to record the environmental, social, political and cultural life of the island. To all, Patmos is, primarily, the island of St. John the Theologian. **In the first half of the 17th century,** the accounts of all those travellers who really came to know the island coincide: the place is arid, there is terrace cultivation and the soil is imported, the ports are very good, the inhabitants make their living by shipping (there are approximately 40 boats in 1610 at which time 7 are sold to the Venetians) and by transporting goods to Italy, mainly the port of Ancona, from Asia Minor (cotton, wax, hide, grain). They bring back to the island all that it requires. The community of Patmos gains prestige. The inhabitants are all Greek ''the richest in these waters''

13

6. Courtyard of the Monastery (p. 31).

(Stochove, 1630), and live in the town of Chora. The population is, approximately, 1000-1200 in 1630, or, according to Thevenot (1655), who gets his imformation second hand, 3000. This is the century of intense building activity both in the Monastery and in Chora. In Scala there are only few storehouses. The pirates find shelter on the island:

7. Iconostasis of the main Church (p. 33).

they take water supplies, mend their ships. As a matter of fact, De Brèves, in 1605, accused the Patmiots as being the worst pirates after the Samians, plunderning Christian and Turk alike! Chora is now full of beautiful houses, the monastery "very beautiful and built like a castle" has 150 monks, an income of 2.000 piastres from Crete and bells — rare privilege in those days. The Church has many objects in silver and "cases full of holy relics" and great collections of sacred articles from different christian places (1610). The island pays to the pasha of Rhodes 4.000 piastres yearly and 500 sequins to the Cadi of Chios (1630). The travellers note the nobility of its inhabitants and the hospitality of its monks. It is stated somewhere that religious painting (icons) flourishes here (1613). Paintings of local painters like those of "Theodoros the priest and notary" still survive.

This first period of prosperity reaches its acme when the Venetian fleet decides to use the port of Scala as a winter anchor-ground, during the great war with the Turks for the occupation of Crete (1645-1669). The presence of the fleet there and the provisions it required helped in making the Patmiots rich. Chora has now, according to Georgirinis, 800 houses. Though the number seems somewhat exaggerated it is not far from the truth. However, this period soon reaches its close with the **destruction of the island by the Venetians** (1659). A brief yet accurate description of the horrors is preserved in codex 107 (f. 30): "In the 18th of June 1659, the Venetian fleet came and pillaged Patmos, it was Saturday, the admiral was one Frasesco (sic) Morosine the Sgardellis, and may he be accursed". In 1671, a traveller writes: "...but since that time, the Turk on the one hand, and the Privateers on the other, have brought them so low that now they are as miserable as any". "And their merchant ships", adds Georgirinis in 1677, "have been reduced to small fishing boats, and the inhabitants to penury". Chora declines. In 1688 Dapper, who reports on hearsay, writes "of many ruins and destroyed houses that one sees in many parts of the town". The christian pirates, who are more ruthless than the Turk, take away all the livestock (1671) and belongings of the monks and islanders. The Turks deprive the Monastery of its cretan possessions, the monks are reduced to penury and turn for help to all directions (Rome, Vlachia, etc.). When Crete succumbs to the Turk (1669) about 50 Cretan families settle in Chora, east of the Monastery, because even in 1665, Patmos is still considered subject to the Venetians. As in the older days (1453), when families from Constantinople (appr. 100) had settled to the south of the Monastery, fleeing the Turks, so now families arrive from Crete. The century closes with a new, long-lasting conflict between the Turks and the Venetians (1684-1718).

During the entire period of Turkish rule the Patriarchate recognises and renews the Monastery's privileges and extends its help in times of hardship. In spite of the fact that the farms and monastic holdings (metochia) are not being cultivated to advantage, they, nevertheless, increase in number. The times are hard, the distances great, leases are not honoured. The Monastery now has holdings in all islands of the Aegean: Paros, Melos, Kea, Samos, Kalymnos, Thera, Naxos, Sifnos, Icaria, Amorgos, Nissiros, and even in Smyrna and Zakynthos. The foreign rulers issue letters of protection and grant subsidies. The faithful, give donations. During this period the Popes: Gregory XIII (1573, 1575), Paul V (1614), Urban VIII (1631), Innocent XI (1681), as well as the kings: Charles VI (1727), Cossimo II, great duke of Etrouria (1674), Victor Amedeus (1682), and other great dignitaries of the order of the Hospitalers (1588; 1610; 1613; 1701) grant protection to the Monastery — though its effectiveness is doubtful. Also, during this period, the princes of Moldavia (1584), of Vlachia (1670) and the tsar of Russia begin to subsidize regularly the Monastery and its holdings. This is especially the case from the 18th century onwards. The orthodox kingdoms along the Danube and in Russia offer help by

8. Patmos after Buondelmondi, 1406 (p. 12).

9. Patmos after G. Rosaccio, 1518 (p. 12).

collection which is carried out by representatives of the Monastery and of its Metochia. When the demands of the conqueror, the political situation and sharp drop in income led the Monastery to an impasse, monks supplied with letters of recommendation (from the Patriarch, their Superior, from the ecclesiastical and govermental authorities of the countries to which they travelled) would visit a great number of provinces preaching, performing the mass and collecting alms from the faithful. A common religion and traditions, but also the political schemes of rulers, create a great interest and concern for the enslaved christians, and favour the colletion of alms.

The institution of almsgiving spreads also to the catholic countries (Italy, Malta). The magistrates ruling in the Dodecanese until 1522, continue to show interest for the Monastery even after Patmos has been occupied by the Turks and give letters of recommendation to the monks who travel around the West seeking help. Of a similar purpose, that is, aiming at economical support for the enslaved orthodox christians in the Turkish Empire, were the so-called "alms-boxes in Asia Minor" for the Monastery (Codex 76).

The situation improved in the beginning of the **18th century.** The population, according to A. De La Montraye (1698), is approximately 4000. There are 93 monks in the Monastery and over one hundred churches in the island. Tournefort (1710/12) says that there are 300 men and twenty times as many women (!) in the island of Patmos. There are 12 caiques and other smaller boats for transporting grain from Asia Minor and the Black Sea which is then re-loaded on French ships. Of the 100 monks resident in the Monastery 40 are occupied with work in the "metochia" of neighbouring isles. The Monastery has an income of 6.000 scudi and a considerable amount of beautiful silver. The turks show respect for the island and the pirates continue to use it for shelter. The island is rich in game, produces some wheat and barley and about 1000 barrels of wine which does not suffice for the island's needs (this fact has been noted earlier, in 1677). Tournerfort is impressed with the beauty of the houses — an inheritance from the good old days which, now, appears disproportionate to the island's reduced state. The domed churches, which according to him are about 250, also impress him. He notes that the administration of the island is in the hands of two Elders who are elected annually and whose responsibility it is to pay the annual taxes (1000 scudi). Here, we should examine two figures given by Tournefort and which seemed to have made a great impression on him: indeed, the number of women on the island is greater than that of men (four or five time, but not twenty) because the women never leave their homes, even if their husbands live permanently elsewhere visiting them once or twice a year. Moreover, they have personal property because the custom is for daughters and not sons to inherit their parents. This enables the women to live far from their husbands. The churches are, as a rule, small, simple and privately owned chapels which function once, or twice a year. The number given by Tournefort is somewhat exaggerated (see below). The picture changes radically around 1720 as a new era of growth begins. An important factor in the island's history is the division which is now effected between the Monastery and the wealthy class of the community. Impressions recorded by travellers seem to agree. In 1741, the Russian Barskij writes: "This is a poor island [...], yet rich in honour and glory, famous not only in the neighbouring areas, but also in the West, because these islanders are first rate merchants and own ships and travel to Venice and Rome and other Latin countries and speak fluently the

10. The Hospitality of Abraham, fresco (p. 37).

11. Christ's anointment at the grave, fresco (p. 38).

foreign languages. They have the custom of wearing rich and elegant clothes, especially the women [...] and the island has about 500 houses which are lovely and very well built, with comfortable interiors, decorated with many vases, mirrors and icons, as is the custom here. Inside, the houses are very clean and white [...] the island suffers frequently from pirate raids[...] yet not so badly because when the pirates come the inhabitants find shelter in the Monastery [...]. The men on this island are either sailors, or merchants. The women weave cotton blankets and rugs and sell them to the merchants who come here, and no one surpasses them in the art of embroidering clothes...''.

R. Pococke, writing eight years later, confirms and completes the picture: "There are seven hundred houses in the town, but only a hundred and sixty persons that pay the poll tax, except those that belong to the convent, who are about two hundred, most of the inhabitants being natives of other places. The convent pays two purses yearly to the captain bashaw for the island. Though the abbot has all the power; yet for the government of the people there are four vicardi for life, who are generally succeeded by their sons. The inhabitants,who are all Christians, are mariners, or shipwrights; for the island is a barren rock, and everything is brought from without. The only export is cotton stockings to Venice, to which city their ships frequently go: They have a few gardens, and make a little poor wine that will not keep above a month; they have good water; it is a very healthy island, and there has been no plague in it for forty years past, so that one sees many old people; for they are careful to guard against infection, by making vessels perform quarantine which come from infected places. The people here are much civilized by the commerce they have abroad; they are immediately subject to the patriarch; and there are three hundred churches in the island".

During this period, the convent, which has its own special organisation, numbers one hundred monks of which fifty work on the Monastery's metochia. Building construction has been completed and the Monastery acquires its present form. Its silver, relics and chandeliers always draw the admiration of the pilgrims.

During the Turkish occupation, the Monastery becomes a nursery of prelates. Between the years 1576-1833 fifty five are known to have existed. Many prelates from other lands come to Patmos to spend the last years of their lives at the convent, while others, who are in disfavour, are exiled here. The monastery also gives shelter to simple folk, orthodox or muslim and pays ransom to liberate slaves and prisoners of war. These are some of the services rendered to mankind which are not set down by History.

The founding of the **school** by Macarios Kalogheras, which is housed in the Monastery (1713), its growth and renown are closely related with this second renaissance of the island. Famous scholars became teachers there, in the school's first period (1713-1818): Macarios Kalogheras, Gerasimos Byzantios, Daniel Kerameus and others. They created numerous disciples who, subsequently, became in their turn scholars, founders of schools, bishops and even patriarchs, spreading the glory of the patmian school there where they were called to work: Greece, Asia Minor, North Africa, the Balkans, Russia. Instruction lasted for seven years and included theology, ancient Greek, philosophy, Latin, rhetoric and ecclesiastical music. Poor student is received scholarships, or financial aid. The school was supported by donations and endowments from wealthy Greeks, and from subsidies granted by the Monastery for quarters, payment of stuff and the library.

In 1739, Pococke writes: "The convent is a sort of novitiate, or seminary, subject to the great convent, and is governed by a professor, whom they call Didascalos, who has a master under him: They teach the ancient Greek, which they call Hellenike [...], physics, metaphysics, and divinity: They use the grammar of Constantine Laskaris of Constantinople, and the logic of Theophilus Corydaleus, both printed in Venice, and the physics and metaphysics of the latter in manuscript, and the divinity of Georgius Quaresius of Scio, which is likewise in manuscript; they teach in a large school; the master instructs the children in the grammar; and the head professor teaches logic, philosophy and divinity. I was present at their lectures; one of the scholars read, and the professor explained it. This school, and the present professor who governs it, are esteemed the best in all the east; they have about fifty scholars who come from different countries, and the greater part lodge in the two convents, though some of them are in town.

Concerning the founder of the school, **Macarios Kalogheras** (fig. 5) a representative type of a 17th century scholar, the Russian traveller Barskij, who studied under him, gives us an excellent portrait:

Macarios was a true son of Patmos. He had lived in Constantinople for a few years and there served as deacon to the Bishop of Heraclea and learned perfectly ancient Greek and Latin, and was distinguished for his virtuous life. Then he abandoned the Bishop, glory, honours and gain, refused to acquire a title in the ecclesiastical hierarchy, and returned to Patmos, his birthplace, where he settled in the Convent, near the grotto, serving his Lord all day and night as a monk of that great Monastery. He is a virtuous, serene and wise man, shy and innocent, who keeps the fast and loves the pilgrims and is useful and helpful to many. He is very well trained in ecclesiastical music and daily chants piously in church and is also a reader and reads so well that those who hear him are moved profoundly. It is over 12 years that, passing through, he decided to settle in this Convent. And ever since, many people have benefited from his teaching of divinity and philosophy. He founded a school and many disciples gathered around him, not only from Patmos but even from neighbouring isles and lands, and he taught grammar and rhetoric, philosophy and theology, Greek and Latin, and he transformed many a fisherman and peasant into philosophers and theologians [...]. And one finds them not only here, but scattered in other lands where the teaching of greek grammar and philosophy has spread since the year 1720. In 1729, thanks to the efforts of the famous teacher Macarios, and the funds provided by a rich man from Constantinople, a larger school was founded on the model of a convent with cells for the scholars from abroad [...] and many do come and study, not only the sons of poor folk, but of high dignitaries from Constantinople, Salonica and Corfu, Crete, Cyprus and various other places. And before, the island of Patmos was deserted and unknown, but now it is famous all over christendom, because this school is to the enslaved Greeks who bear the Turkish yoke, a substitute for ancient Athens".

The information we have from travellers concerning **the second half of the 18th century** is very scant. Information of more recent date (1816) states that the mariners of Patmos, as of 1769, enjoy French protection. Choiseul-Gouffier, who made the best prints of the island (see figs. 1, 3) informs us that the Monastery had in those days (1776-85) 80 monks. Mention is made of the great financial difficulties

12. St. Chariton, fresco (p. 38).

faced by the Monastery in the 2nd half of the 18th and the beginning of the 19th century. W. Wittman, who visited the island for a few hours, repeats the previous observations: that the houses which are about 200 are well made, that terrace cultivation yields a poor crop, that the number of women far surpasses that of men. During the Russian-Turkish war (1768-1774), the Russians who had a division of their fleet anchored at Scala, commandeer four big merchant ships belonging to the island. In answer to a Russian letter, the Patmiots compose their first surviving census and inventory (1773). According to this source, the population is 2086 inhabitants: 124 "monks and clergy", 40 nuns, 140 resident foreigners and 1786 natives (1040 women and 411 children). The island has 510 inhabited houses, 49 horsemills, 4 windmills of which only one is in operation, and about 150 churches. Crops suffice for one, maximum two months and, therefore, everything has to be imported. Export is restricted to

13. St. Cyprianos, fresco (p. 38). →

Ο ΑΓΙΟC ΚΥ ΠΡΙ Α ΝΟC

pottery and stockings (made with cotton from Kusandasi). Taxes rise to 1092 grossia of which the monastery covers 1/3. As for capital tax, the village pays 4/5 and the monastery 1/5. Evidence for the growth and prosperity of the island during this century comes from numerous sources. K. Krumbacher who visited the island in 1886 writes: "Even during the previous century, Patmos had a large, merchant fleet composed of excellent ships which were in continuous contact with England, Holland and Italy. Her trade, in those days, was, relatively speaking, as important as that of Chios and Smyrna [...]. In some of the old houses I saw expensive pieces of dutch furniture, good and bad venetian and dutch paintings, antique clocks and other remnants of the past. I counted altogether no less than 70 paintings of the 17th and 18th centuries". Similar impressions are recorded by G. Tischendorf (1859) and C. Newton (1853).

In the beginning of **the 19th century,** the traveller E.D. Clarke (1811/13) is the first to note down information concerning the Monastery's library from which, incidentally, he took a few, but very valuable manuscripts. Also, he gives shorter descriptions about the islands's boats (12) which transport corn between the Euxine and Italy, and mentions the pirates who continue to use the island as shelter, taking water supplies and repairing their ships there — a long, inescapable symbiosis for the islanders. Shortly before the revolution (1816) W. Turner first notes that Scala has now about 50 houses, besides shops: "...the men are all seamen and making frequent voyages to the ports of Europe, in their employer's sevice, they get the habits of Franks (whose dress is very common among them) and are more enlightened and far less superstitious than the majority of the Greeks [...] The chief employment of the women is in making cotton stockings, of which their boats import the materials from Anatolia. Their stockings are famed throughout the Levant for their durability..." Turner notes that in the last years the Turks forbid the Patmiots to be under French protection, that the island is subject to the jurisdiction of captain pasha and pays to him a yearly tax of 2.000 piastres. Few years later, R. Walpole counts 240 churches, 589 inhabited houses and 52 resident monks (1820).

Patmos' trade expansion had as a direct consequence the formation of many flourishing trading communities in the Balkans, Austria, Russia and Egypt. It is to these communities and the School of Patmos that modern Greece owes the appearance of those inspired men who led the **War of Independence (1821-1828).** Among them, we distinguish the patriarch of Alexandria Theophilos Pancostas, E. Xanthos, founder of the revolutionary organisation "Philiki Hetaireia" and Demetrios Themelis, who died at the siege of Mesolonghi. Patmos took an active part in the struggle by joining on the 1st of May, 1821. Yet, with the treaty of Constantinople (9.7.1832) Patmos was once again subjected to the Turks, until 1912 when the Italians took over. A census taken during the Revolution (1827) gives us a good picture of the then flourishing community: there are 652 men of which 52 are merchants; 25 workshop owners; 10 Aï class captains and 25 Bï class captains; 252 sailors; 21 potters; 68 farmers;21 fishermen; 20 sheperds. There are yet: 4 smiths; 3 painters; five musicians (vocal and instrumental music); 3 doctors; 2 teachers and the Consul of Britain. Participation in the War of Independence was not without cost. G. Emerson speaks of the desolation and poverty of the place -every little scrub had to be cut because the ships could not carry the timber necessary for building and the wood necessary for fuel. Yet, even after this hard period Patmos continues to live with its old rythm, though not with its old wealth. The picture given by L. Ross (1841) reminds us of previous accounts: "In general, Patmos surpasses in wealth and education the neighbouring isles and this is due, in part to the Monastery and its school, in part to the highly developed trade of the island... Many Patmiots serve in the Greek administration, some in the Russian, while others live as merchants in Smyrna and Constantinople. The population is about 4000 souls. There are 300 seamen who have about 12 clippers and schooners and other smaller boats". The island's income rises to 150.000 francs (if one excludes the returns from maritime activities), and is derived from the exportation of knitted stockings (100.000 drachmas gross income yearly), pottery which is produced in the workshops of Scala (first mentioned in 1773) and shipped to Smyrna, Rhodes and Alexandria. Fishing and agriculture also contribute to the island's income. Patmos has a few gardens and vineyards, a few scattered farms where corn is grown, some olive trees. The island continues to pay tax to the pasha of Rhodes. The rapid growth of Scala, which in 1848 has 100 houses, cafés, shops and pottery workshops, points to the fact that times have changed: piracy declines and the inhabitants are not afraid anymore to live near the shore. Yet, pirates still roam the seas. C. Tischendorf who is the first person to undertake a systematic study of the Convent's Library (1846) reports that he was afraid of the pirates while travelling from Samos to Patmos. The Monastery has, during this time, a small number of monks that varies (30 to 50 from 1834-1889). Most of them live on the monastic farms. All the monks are Patmiots — an old tradition since every family considered it a privilege to have a representative in the Monastery. A landmark in the Convent's spiritual history is the systematic organisation of its library, which is undertaken during this period. R. Burgess (1834) and L. Ross (1841) both mention this fact. The library attracts now the attention of European specialists like Tischendorf (1846 and 1859), Krumbacher (1886) and the greek I. Sakkelion. The monks of the Monastery study as well the documents and codices (I. Florides, G. Papazoglou).

By the end of the 19th century, Patmos has fallen again into obscurity. K. Krumbacher, who stayed some time on the island (1886) speaks of 2000 inhabitants who, in one way or another, depend on the Monastery for their living. J. Bute, a year earlier, speaks of 1000 inhabitants who are all very poor. The men emigrate to Odessa, Smyrna, Constantinople and Alexandria. The island's boats have now a reduced area of activity: they transport grain and bulls from the south of Asia Minor to Samos and Pireus. From Syros, they load european, industrial products and carry them to the Sporades and Patmos. The school is deserted. Krumbacher gives us the best and fullest description of the age-old industry of stockings which constituted the main occupation of women in Patmos: "Even today, and inspite of factory antagonism, the famous hand industry of stockings is the main source of income for Patmos. All the women, that is, about 1000, for the greatest part of the year, during the day and often during the night, hold in their hands their stocking needles and knit [...]. Only the little children do not work at this trade [...]. Small schools for knitting have been formed so that the younger generation may quickly learn this craft [...]. Older girls and women also gather and form numerous knitting groups [...]. While knitting, the women sing folk songs which, sometimes, the air carries from the workshops up to the Monastery's ramparts".

Lay life on the island is affected by many factors. The creation of an independent Greek state has as a consequence the appearance of

Ο ΛΟΥΚΑС

14. St. Mark, illumination, codex 80 (p. 49).

15. Birth of St. John the Baptist, St. Luke, Illumination, codex 274 (p. 49).

new urban and spiritual centres. Changes in the means of transportation, the shift in trading centres and, generally, the new conditions in the Aegean together with the disappearance of the old privileges, prove fatal for the island. With the 20th century, immigration takes the place of trading and shipping activities. In 1912, the Turks cede the Dodecanese islands to the Italians. In 1947 they are united with Greece.

Today, Chora lives through its memories: medieval alley-ways, customs, a certain life-rythm, the language - all speak of the past. A strong religious feeling orders daily life. One sees in Patmos today the survival of certain old, forgotten, orthodox rituals: magnificent Easter ceremonies reminiscent of byzantine times, the feast of "the washing of the feet" and other rituals. The monastery, keeper of the byzantine tradition and treasury of orthodoxy, remains the focal point of the town. Nine centuries of worship and art await the visitor within its high walls.

THE MONASTERY

The Monastery is a fortress. It is one of the finest examples of a medieval, fortified monastery. When the Blessed Christodoulos settled on the island his first concern was to insure the protection of the Monastery by building walls and ramparts: "We, therefore, began immediately to lay the foundations and to build ramparts and walls, urged by one thought, how, the soonest, to protect ourselves by raising them as high as our strength allowed". Piracy and unceasing wars in the area made imperative the building of strong ramparts if the Monastery was to survive. Instructions given by a 12th century abbot concerning protection from the pirates during the summer months, give us a good picture of the situation: "Come May, neve allow the soldiers or any islander to return to their homes. Let them come and stay at the Monastery in order to protect it. Fill the bastions with stones, keep unfailing watch, and fight courageously so as to please God and ourselves".

The exterior of the Monastery is weighty and austere. The ground-plan of the **fortification** is polygonal and its largest dimensions 70×53 metres. It is composed of bare, vertical walls (the openings are of a later date) strengthened at the base (17th century) by a steep escarpment. High towers protect it. The walls are crowned with battlements. There is a bastion [4] in front of the main gate (see ground-plan inside front cover and follow numbers in brackets).

We mount the wide, ascending pathway whose steps lead to the Monastery's entrance [1]. It was constructed by the abbot Nichephoros the Cretan in 1603 who also constructed the chapel of the Holy Apostles [3]. Moving to the left of the gate, we can easily make the tour of the Monastery. Forty years ago, the open space which now surrounds the Monastery was filled with the older houses of Chora. A narrow street divided them for defense purposes from the fortification. High up, on the NE and NW side we note five inscriptions with the names of benefactors who made donations for further strengthening of the walls and of the escarpment (1601-1700): Nicolas Mathas (1652) who came from an old, patmian family, and the Archbishop of Carpathos, Neophytos Grymanis (1700). Two machicolations also survive, one in the middle of the eastern side and another in the middle of the southern, right over a small iron gate

16. The Monastery after Barskij, 1730 (p. 18).

which opened rarely and only when absolutely needed. (The western range of the fortification has been restored according to the old plan). Before the main gate we see the **chapel of the Holy Apostles** [3] typical specimen of the architectural style of those days. It combines a traditional style mixed with late gothic and renaissance influences that have come from Crete (1603).

The **main entrance** [5] was protected by two towers, a thick iron gate with a double bar and a machicolation — a projecting platform with an opening from which one could pour boiling oil, or water, or molten lead on those who dared approach it with an evil intent (today only the exterior, northern wall stands). The gate was placed under the protection of St. John the Theologian who figures in a fresco painted in a niche above the gate. An archway [6] leads from the gate to the central courtyard. The guard lived "right next to the gate" (left of the archway).

The Monastery was constructed without an original, uniform plan and is, therefore, composed of **buildings** dating from various periods. The main church was erected in the days of the Blessed Christodoulos, the Refectory and cells in the 12th century. Some of the cisterns which are to be found under the courtyard and the main church also date from this period. Donations for buildings were given principally by Neophytos Grymanis of Carpathos (1698-1700) and Nectarios of Sardis (end of 18th, beginning of 19th century). As yet, we do not possess a complete architectural study of the Monastery. The

ὁ ἅγιος ΜΑΡΚΟϹ

+ ἘΚ ΤΟΥ ΜΑΡ⳽

ὦ μαι ἐρρῶ κεῖμαι⳽ ἐ
πορεύετο ὀῖϲ ἐμ τοῖϲ
σάμμασι διὰ τῶμ
σπορίμωμ, καὶ οἱ
ξαμ τοῖϲ μαθηταὶ

18. *St. Luke, illumination, codex 81 (p. 49).*

buildings rest on the inner flank of the protective wall and are separated by courtyards which provide light and air. Cells, chambers, chapels, storerooms — all communicate through a network of passages, arcades and stairways. They are all picturesque, white and very clean but often... problematical. For, the place is a veritable labyrinth!

← *17, St. Mark, illumination, codex 75 (p. 49).*

The central courtyard [7] paved with pebbles and decorated with arches constitutes the centre of the Monastery (fig. 6). The north and west sides are enclosed by the white walls of the cells. To the south rises a two-storied arcade built of dressed stone (1698). To the east, the courtyard is enclosed by the outer narthex of the main church [8] in front of which was erected, at a much more recent date, the four-arched arcade which supports by means of three great arches the western wall opposite. It is here that the great, wooden simandron and the small iron simandron hang. On feast days, five monks beat rythmically upon the first before the chiming of the bells. Upon entering the courtyard, to the left we can see the tomb of Gregory of Cos, bishop of Didimotichon (†January, 1693). Carved inscriptions inform us that the Patmiot Patriarch Neophytos, who died in March, 1747, is also buried here. In the centre of the courtyard, the large, circular stone pedestal encloses an enormous, old wine-jar which, in the old days, was carefully sealed and entrusted to the care of a monk "... graced with sobriety and steadfastness" (today it contains holy water). The jars placed at the SW side of the courtyard served for collecting the rain water falling from the roof. The mouth of the well, set near the west wall, communicates with the cisterns which are under the courtyard. Near the SE entrance, to the right of the niche where the Blessed Founder is painted, we see encased in the wall some fragments of early christian architectural sculptures.

THE MAIN CHURCH

The main church is to the east of the central courtyard and leans against the protective wall. It was completed at about 1090. The **outer narthex** [8] was built in the 17th century and is composed of an open, four-arched arcade. The materials come from the older christian church which stood on the same site (4th century). The ruins of the older church in the midst of which stood a little chapel, were discovered by "the scribe of the Cyclades" when he presented Christodoulos with the island: "... a little chapel in honour of the Theologian built, as the ruins make clear, on the site where once a magnificent church stood on the summit of the highest mountain". The lower part of the eastern wall of the outer narthex is covered with frescoes of a poor quality that were painted during the last century (1891). The vaulting is also decorated with frescoes, the oldest and best dating from the 17th century. The themes illustrated come from "The Travels and Miracles of St. John the Theologian" (see p. 9). Over the main entrance we can see the Miracle of the Ressurection of the Young Domnos at Ephessus. To the right, the Miracle of the Salvation of the young man who fell overboard the ship transporting enchained St. John and Prochoros to their exile in Patmos. Over the entrance which leads to the Chapel that enshrines the relics of the Founder, we can see the drowning of the magician Cynops. Higher up, on the southern wall, the burial of St. John and other representations based on the text. The three, external, wooden doors through which the outer narthex communicates with the inner narthex [10] and the chapel of the Blessed Christodoulos [9], date from the 17th century. Of interest is the floor of the outer narthex which is paved with warm-coloured, marble slabs forming simple, geometrical patterns.

From the outer narthex we enter the **Chapel of the Blessed Christodoulos** [9] which was built (16th cent.) on the south corner of the 12th century older narthex. Its iconostasis has three icons dating from the beginning of the 17th century: Christ, the Virgin, and the Blessed Founder. The frescoes are of a more recent date and seriously damaged. On the south side there is a niche which contains what could be the original, marble sarcophagus of the Founder. On the sarcophagus rests a wooden casket containing the relics of the holy man. The cover and front part are silver-gilt and imprinted with representations: on the cover, the crucifixion and the four Evangelists; on the front, the burial of the Blessed Founder; in the centre and on the sides, St. John and his disciple Prochoros. The work was done in 1796 in a Smyrna workshop (fig. 29).

From the north entrance of the chapel (carved, wooden door dating from the end of the 15th, beginning of 16th century) we come to the **inner narthex** [10] which is covered by a semi-circular dome. The eastern side is supported by a big arch which rests on two, half-buried early christian columns. The floor is paved with black and white marble slabs of which the central is decorated with a multi-coloured, rectangular border. The frescoes, damaged in part and blackened by smoke, belong to different periods, the most recent dating from 1803. On the west (from S to N) we can see the Massacre of the Innocents, the meeting of St. Elizabeth and the Virgin, the Adoration of the Magi. The best preserved fresco is on the north wall depicting the Parable of the Wise and Foolish Virgins. On the vaulted roof we can faintly distinguish the 12 Apostles with Christ in the centre. The icon of St. John the Theologian placed to the right of the entrance leading to the main nave, is the palladium of the Monastery. The halo and gospel are later additions. Today, we can only distinguish from the original work (the icon was repainted in the 19th century) the gilt frame which is decorated with 13th century medallions representing Jesus Christ, the Virgin, St. John the Baptist and the Apostles. Next to the icon we note a beautiful icon-stand decorated with ivory and mother-of-pearl, bearing the inscription: "Hatziconsta (son) of Spanos from Sime, 1698".

From the main entrance whose carved door (late 15th, early 16th century) is surmounted by an ancient marble lintel, we enter the **church proper** [11] where later additions on all sides hide its original aspect (see fig. 34). The nave is in the form of a greek cross inscribed on a square over which rises a dome supported by four columns two of which are behind the iconostasis. The floor is paved with decorated, marble slabs. The original 17th century frescoes are covered by more recent ones which were painted in the early 19th century and then re-painted at the end of the same century. On the north wall recent restoration has brought to light samples of the older frescoes. Below these, it is probable that there is another, earlier series of frescoes dating from the byzantine period and corresponding to those we see in the chapel of the Virgin.

The iconostasis (fig. 7), completed in 1820 and donated by the Patmiot metropolitan Nectarios of Sardis is heavy and disproportionate in relation to the small size of the church. It is filled with scenes from the Bible. This iconostasis replaced an earlier, wooden one which, at some earlier time, had replaced the original stone iconostasis erected by the Blessed Christodoulos. The icons date from various periods: St. Jonh the Divine (1697), Jesus Christ (1709), the Virgin (all three painted in Russia) and St. James the Zebedee "by the hand of James Ioasaf, in 1843". The Superior's throne is ornamented with inlaid, mother-of-pearl floral motifs. The inscription it bears refers to the pious donor; "Remember, O Lord, Thy servant

19. St. Nicholas, mosaic icon (p. 56).

the Arch-priest Gregory; in the year 1694''. Near the columns stand two lecterns decorated with inlaid bands of ivory. Engraved inscriptions set in ivory commemorate the donor: ''Grymanis Neophytos, 1696, humble Bishop of Carpathos, 1696''. Two reading desks ornamented with ivory, mother-of-pearl and tortoise shell, as well as a number of old, silver chandeliers and oil lamps, which drew

20. St. James, icon (p. 56).

the admiration of many travellers, complete the decoration of the church. Of particular interest are the icons painted by well-known artists, among them Emmanuel Tzanes (1674).

On the north wall, near the sanctuary, a large icon of the Apocalypse (1625, presented to the church by Nicephoros, Bishop of Laodicea), hides the entrance to the **outer treasury** [12] a small room

21. Virgin enthroned, fresco (p. 37).

constructed in 1625 by Nicephoros himself for the safe keeping of his books. This we learn from an inscription carved above the inner side of the entrance. Today, in this room the Monastery keeps a large number of its precious possessions: vestments, crosses, mitres, bishops' staffs, candlesticks, etc. **The ancient treasury** lies behind the sanctuary [13]. It is not open to visitors. There, the Monastery keeps its treasures: silver lamps and censers, candlesticks, numerous icons, saintly relics and pieces from the True Cross. The relics (over sixty in number) are encased in precious reliquaries with representations of the saints, inscriptions and additional decorations engraved or imprinted, inlaid with mother-of-pearl and ornamented with enamel and filigree work, sometimes with pearls and precious stones. A number of these surviving relics are mentioned in the Treasury's first catalogue which dates from 1200, namely, of St. James of Persia, of St. Stephen the younger and of the holy Apostle Philip the Deacon. These holy relics constitute a tangible evidence of the life, death and miracles of the saints and martyrs of Orthodoxy and, therefore, Monasteries consider them their most treasured possessions. From the earliest centuries of the christian era to acquire them was something very difficult, to possess them, a true blessing as their benificent influence on all aspects of private and public life was considered decisive.

The chapel of the Virgin [14] is small (8.40×33.05 m) and covered with a groined, semi-cylindrical vault. It was built in the 12th century. It is paved with marble slabs. A stone with a half-effaced, ancient greek inscription forms the threshold of the central door of the iconostasis, and an early christian capital carved with pigeons can be seen on one of the columns supporting the arch of the northern wall. The beautiful, wooden iconostasis (1607) which replaced an older, marble one, is adorned with old icons. The murals were painted in 1185-90 and covered in 1745 (see inscription over entrance) by other mediocre ones (see as an example The Virgin of the Heavens on the ceiling of the Refectory). Restoration undertaken in 1958 brought to light the original ones. The serenity and nobility of the pose; the austerity of expression; the symmetry of the composition; the absence of realistic, background detail (landscapes, or buildings) and the express monotony in the arrangement of the themes, give to these representations an appearance of deep solemnity and divine austerity. This impression is not affected by the geometrical style, the roughness of the line or the strong lighting. In the lower section of the eastern wall, where the frescoes are preserved intact, we can see the Lady of the Angels Enthroned with Christ on Her knees (fig. 21). On either side stand the austere Archangels Michael and Gabriel dressed in imperial robes and holding banners. Above, we see Abraham's Hospitality (Genesis, 18, 1-2) a symbolic representation of the Trinity (fig. 10). On the west wall, where the frescoes are relatively well preserved, we can see representations of St. John Chrysostomos, fountain of wisdom, and above, the Miracle of the Healing of the Infirm Woman (Luke 3, 11-12). On the south wall, to the left the representation of the Virgin in the Temple, and above, a section of the Healing of the Paralytic (John 5, 2-9). Finally, on the north wall, over the sanctuary, the meeting of Christ with the Samaritan Woman (John 4, 4-7). On the ceiling, sections of other compositions survive. The remaining surfaces are covered with representations of saints. Below, stand the eastern prelates from Jerusalem, tall, gaunt, white-bearded figures holding with one hand the Gospel and with the other blessing. The noblest form among them is that of St. James, brother of Christ (NE corner). The upper sections of the walls and a section of the dome are decorated with medallions of saints blessing, or martyrs holding the cross. It is interesting to note the differences in the style of the figures, their clothes and poses as well as the colours used: a painterly technique is employed to depict the young saints and martyrs, a linear for the old ones.

The quality and extent of this work which was executed at a time when both the Monastery and the Empire were undergoing great difficulties, suggests the idea that a person of high standing who had intimate connections with the Monastery must have financed it. The special preference of the painter for the prelates from Jerusalem, which he painted towards the end of the 12th century, allows us to think that the donor may have been Leo, Patriarch of Jerusalem (1176-1185/90). Leo, a member of the Monastery's brotherhood since his youth, was a Superior there from 1157/8 and held the office until 1183 concurrently with the patriarchal title (1176).

Indicative of the support which the brotherhood expected from him who rose to the highest ranks, is the complaint which they lodged when Leo refused the throne "of the metropolitan of Russia" and the Archbishopry of Cyprus: "It seems to us, Father, that you do not care either for yourself or for us, who look to you as second to God, neither do you wish to benefit the Monastery [...] because our Monastery willgrow and in many ways flourish".

The Refectory [15] is the place where the monks have their communal meals. It was completed around 1090. The building is rectangular (6.32×6.60 m) and had, originally, a wooden, inclining ceiling. A semi-circular room towards the eastern side, probably served as a pantry (16). The barell-vaulted roof, the dome and the inner butresses date from the 12th or 13th century. In the centre of the Refectory are two long, built - in tables covered with marble and decorated round the sides, where we can see small hollows carved for the placing of personal belongings (knife, pewter, etc.), with an interlacing pattern.

The frescoes were done in three stages (numbers in brackets refer to the diagramme of representations on the inside of the back cover). The first series were painted in the beginning of the 13th century when the building had an inclining roof. We can see in the recess of the blind arches of the west wall frescoes of saints [1, 2, 3, 4] and scenes [5, 6, 7, 8]. The figures of the saints (see fig. 12) are more lively in movement and expression than those in the chapel. To the second phase (first half of 13th century) belong the representations of the northern section of the west wall: Saints standing as prototypes of virtue [a, b, c, 9] in the lower frieze (fig. 13) and above [10, 12] scenes relevant to the use for which the room was intended. The style is highly formalised and particular attention is given to the folding of gowns and other details. The liveliness in movement and, especially, the representation of Judas from the back [12] as well as the rendering of the disciples from a raised perspective in the next scene [13] constitute important differences in relation to the style and technique of the previous phase. The third phase (second half of 13th century) is characterised by the frescoes painted on the transversal aisle of the southern section [d-e, and 18-26]. They are not well preserved because of the bad quality of the paints that were used. Here we have scenes of passion (fig. 11) and dogmatic themes. The style is less formal and more realistic in the depiction of expressive, emotional states: the fainting of the Virgin at the Crucifixion [18], Mary pulling her hair in despair at the Mourning over the Tomb [21]. Noteworthy is the painter's attempt to use perspective in the background [21]. Of special interest are the scenes depicting the second [24], fourth [25] and sixth Oecumenical Synods. Facing each other, stand the groups of the Orthodox and of the Heretics, who are deprived of haloes and their gowns are plain. The leaders hold open scrolls upon which their opposed views are written. It is quite possible that on the opposite walls the remaining Synods were depicted (1st, 3d, 5th, 7th).

Today, we can see in the Refectory a collection of ancient

22. St. Theodore of Tyre (p. 56). →

inscriptions found on the island, and a beautiful section of an ionian capital. Early christian architectural fragments and byzantine reliefs are also on exhibition, as well as the surviving part of an old inscription commemorating the completion of the great church that had been erected in that older period: "the inauguration took place..." On the upper part of the walls we can see the frescoes that were painted in the chapel of the Virgin in 1745, and which were subsequently removed to reveal the original ones.

For the specialist and all those who wish to have a more intimate view of the Monastery's daily life, **the remaining rooms** are of considerable interest. They do not present any special artistic attraction yet their functional simplicity constitutes, together with other surviving similar buildings, a valuable source of information concerning monastic and, more generally, popular byzantine architecture. From the Refectory we come to the **kitchen** [17] (see ground-plan on front cover) which was completed in 1091, the ovens are topped with domes. Tradition places under the roofed space [18] the mill. However, no trace survives to justify such a view.

From the central courtyard [7], going through the gate which is on the ground floor below the southerm arcade, we come to the **cellars** [19]. The temperature there is cool enough to insure the preservation of foodstuff. A narrow passage leads to the vaulted "orion" where wheat and dried vegetables were stored. A domed cistern built in the shape of a jar (base 2.60, height 2.20) takes up the lower half of this room (see diagram on back cover). We can only see the circular opening of this cistern in the centre of the raised floor (diam. 0.87) because the space intervening between the walls and its sides has been filled to ensure the preservation of its contents by making it air-tight. The adjoining cellar was for the storing of oil **(pithones).** This was kept in huge jars set in rows against the walls and half-buried in the ground. For the preservation, storing and management of foodstuff the Monastery's Rule appoints a Cellarer "to be chosen from among the brotherhood for his piousness, long experience and aptitude to undertake this office. He shall have two assistants and a cook under his orders" (for a visit to the cellars, a special permit is required). To insure the Monastery's water supply, **cisterns** which take up almost the entire area under the Monastery were constructed at an early time. These cisterns connect with the mouth of the wells from which, even today, fresh, pure water can be drawn to serve the Monastery's needs. The cisterns, insulated with water-proof rough-cast, have vaulted ceilings and the largest ones also have arch supports. Earthen pipes carry the water from the roof terraces, which are carefully cleaned before the raining season, to the cisterns. The cisterns are kept clean thanks to a special opening on their ceiling and a draining pipe at their base. At the western end of the second level of the arcade that runs along the south side of the central courtyard, if we turn left and descend five steps we come to the **Bakery.** Here the bread was prepared and baked. We can see the enormous kneading-through hewn out of a single plane tree (3.60 × 0.80 h.0.60) and at the far end of the room two domed brick ovens (one of the ovens in on view in the exhibition halls).

The northern entrance to the Bakery gives access to an inner courtyard where the **chapel** dedicated **to All Saints** is to be seen (17th century). A small belfry on the south side marks its position. Opposite the entrance stand the oldest cells of the Monastery in two floors (12th century). The cells [21] are fairly large (2.70x4.55), vaulted, and have niches and fireplaces cut into the thick walls. On the terrace above the southern arcade we see the **chapel of the Holy Cross** (1598) an almost cubical construction of dressed, grey stone surmounted by a large dome. The only decoration on the exterior walls is a window over the entrance with an oriental arch. It has a simple, wooden iconostasis with old icons representing Our Lady of the Angels, the Crucifixion and the Finding and Raising of the Holy Cross. The **chapel of St. John the Baptist** is on the same level, over the inner courtyard. **The chapel of St. Basil** is situated below and to the right of the steeple; its dome is semi-cylindrical. Some interesting parts of frescoes survive, f.e., the Ascension, and St. Basil "painted by the hand of Daniel", as well as an inscription. On the plastered walls we note some graffiti of various types of vessels —a memory that is preserved to remind us of the island's maritime past. The **chapel of St. Nicholas** lies behind the dome of the main church. It is topped by a semi-cylindrical dome. Its wooden iconostasis is simple yet adorned with beautiful, old icons.

The **roof terraces** of the Monastery are on different levels, small in size, paved with tiles and surrounded with battlements. They are divided by the tile-covered domes of the chapels and the courtyard openings. Short, white staircases connect them. The roof terrace which is situated on the highest western section of the Monastery offers to the viewer the most **magnificent vista of the island and the Aegean sea** "perhaps, one of the best in the world" (C. Perry, 1743). To the north is the island of Samos, home of Pythagoras. A little to the west the smaller island of Korassiai and Phourni. To the north west stretches Icaria. On very clear days one can see the Cyclades to the west, Mykonos, the islet of Dhonoussa, then Naxos, and in the distance the summits of Paros. To the south west, to the right of the summit of "Prophet Elijah", one can see the mountains of Amorgos. To the south, near Patmos, is Levithos, and farther off Astypalaea. To the south east is Leros, and behind it and a little more to the south Kalymnos and Cos, the home of Hippocrates. Very close to Patmos on the east lies the island of Hiliomodi and beyond it Lipsos. To the north east are the islets of Arki, and beyond them Agathonissi. From Leros to Samos we can distinguish in the horizon the coastline of Asia Minor where the double summit of Mount Mycale rises. The horizon, the sea, the rocks constantly change in colour and shape.

Sunset is the most beautiful moment: an unforgettable memory of a purple world, and an intense feeling of solitude and strength created by the immeasurable, calm expanse.

THE LIBRARY

The Monastery of Patmos houses one of the most important Libraries in the East. Today, it contains about 1.000 manuscripts (325 on parchment and 565 on paper) and over 3.000 volumes of printed books.

Founder of the Library was the Blessed Christodoulos. His one concern was to preserve and to increase (by purchase and copying) the codices which he subsequently bequeathed to the Monastery. The instructions he gave to his successors concerning the preservation of this treasure from every official or other covetousness — "and the sacristan should undertake the preservation and with diligence guard the books and codices of the Monastery and everything else that

23. The Assumption of the Virgin (p. 56).

belongs to the church" — won him a place of honour among those who contributed towards the renaissance of learning in that period. The instructions he gave to the Monastery's scribes are characteristic of his concern: "If a monk is gifted as a calligraphist, he is to work under the direction of the superior... the monastery will supply him with the materials and tools necessary for his work, but as soon as the

24. The Visitation to the Temple (p. 56).

work is completed the new manuscript shall become the property of the Monastery''. The followers of the Founder continued his work and established the great tradition of learning that is associated with the Monastery. They collected and bequeathed to the Monastery codices which, together with the ones copied there or donated by the pious inhabitants of the neighbouring areas (Rhodes, Chios, Crete, etc.)

43

brought the total number up to 330 by the beginning of the 13th century.

We can form a complete picture of what the Library was like at this period by **a catalogue dated 1200** which is preserved in the archives. This catalogue, which is one of the rare surviving library catalogues of the byzantine period (the second one in this Library's history, the first, being a brief one, issued in 1103) is a priceless source of information on the history of byzantine literature and on the intellectual interests of the age. Its loan lists illustrate the extent to which the Library's fame had spread. Though this was a period of great difficulties for the Empire, nevertheless the Monastery continued to be a flourishing intellectual centre, guardian and producer of invaluable texts which were of use not only to the Monastery's "metochia" (Leros, Kos, Asia Minor), but also to neighbouring religious foundations (Asia Minor, Calymnos, Samos) even to private individuals. Of interest is a section of the catalogue listing 30 manuscripts bequeathed to the Monastery by the second successor of the Blessed Christodoulos, the Superior Savas (1127/28) which most probably contains a great number of the Founder's manuscripts.

The contents of the Library at this period are almost exclusively religious in character. Among the 267 codices in parchment, 109 treat of liturgical subjects, 107 contain edifying tales and writings of the Church Fathers, while 31 are hagiographical. There are only 20 non - theological texts and only one among these is a classical text — Aristotle's *Categories*. This collection is characteristic of the intellectual preferences of monks in the 12th century. It is very suitable for such a large monastic establishment and very valuable though limited in scope. The Library today has 111 of these "very ancient" codices of which 108 are on parahment and 3 on paper. Charles Diehl writes: "We should be grateful to the monks of the 11th and 12th centuries who succeeded in combining their religious duties with such noble and serious preoccupations. These win for them a high place in the history of Letters and renders them worthy of our gratitude and respect".

Subsequent catalogues (1262/7, 1307, circa 1335, 1381) together with reports from travellers allow us to trace in a general way **the history of the Library.** This is rather rare for any library of the Medieval period. Between the end of the 12th century, when the monastery was founded, and the end of the 14th century, the number of codices increases steadily. Towards the middle of the 14th century a new spirit seems to have arisen as far as the intellectual interests of monks are concerned: historical and literary works appear as well as the works of classical authors (catalogue 1355) like Diodorus Siculus, Xenophon, Plato. This breadth of outlook is noteworthy as it is rather unusual for a byzantine Monastery. However, by the end of the 14th century the Library begins to show signs of decline: the codices are less carefully guarded and many are never returned by the borrowers. The hard years which followed, greatly reduced the number of old codices especially those of a non-theological nature. The total number stays the same because donations to the Library continue and the Monastery had also acquired the libraries of those monasteries in Asia Minor that had been evacuated after the Turkish occupation. In the 16th century special attention is given to the codices (binding, renovations, etc.). At the beginning of the 17th century, Nicephoros, Bishop of Laodicea, bequeathed his personal library to the Monastery and built the outer treasury as a special place for housing the books.

The acquisition of codices increases steadily until the 18th century when there is an astonishing increase in the number of printed books and a marked decrease in the number of priceless codices which, of cource, is due to the traveller - manuscript hunter, the "editors" who "forget" to return the ancient manuscripts after having consulted them...

Of particular interest for the history of the Library (year, source, scribes of codices) and the sentiments of the owners and donors of texts are the **notes** one finds written **in the codices.** For instance, on the first leaf of Codex 175, dated 1180 (f.1r) we read: "I, Nilos, great sinner, and unlettered peasant, do this little book written by me dedicate to the greatly venerated holy Convent of Patmos, so that the Saint may be mindful of me; not because the Convent is lacking in books — far from me any such thought, for what Monastery worthy of respect has so many scribes and calligraphists as this Monastery built by God and dedicated to him whom the Lord loved. Whosoever would deprive this holy Monastery of this, Nilos' gift, on pretext just or unjust, let him be accursed and damned! So be it! Amen".

In codex 75 (12th century), the prelate who dedicates the book to the Monastery in 1460, writes: "In the year 1460, in the month of September 30th, indiction. I, in humblesse, and out of my own free will, and desire, decided to give and to dedicate to this sacred, venerable Monastery, which is in the island called Patmos, and is the Monastery of my glorious, all-prophetic Apostle and Evangelist John the Theologian, this sacred, holy gospel which is ornamented in the manner it appears, as well as a blue "epitaphios" (liturgical veil) embroidered in thread of gold, and another one in thread of gold but on a purple background; also a triodion book in carta bombycina and a pendicostarion book in carta bombycina for the salvation of my soul. And let no one deprive the Monastery of these my gifts now and in all eternity, for no one has, or ever will have the permission or authority to sell, or exchange, or give them away, in whichever way and at whatever time; and he who would set his heart by any means to deprive the said Monastery of them, may he be damned, as the traitor of our Lord Judas was, and may his soul be damned to dwell with the devils!..."

Another dedicator, codex 853 dated 1494 (f 39), hurls much heavier curses on those who would dare deprive the Monastery of his gift: "... and if one gives to the pupils while at their lessons this book thus causing its destruction, may the curses of the 300 saintly and godly Fathers who were at the Council of Nicene fall upon him, and the leprosy of Gehazi overtake him, and may he have the great St. John the Theologian and the Blessed Father Christodoulos as his accusers on the Day of Judgement..." Other notes commemorate binding or other work done in the Library: "This book was renovated by the hieromonk Athanasius who at the time was sacristan of the Monastery, in the year of our Lord 1754, in October. Let those who assist the sacristan read this edifying Theotokarion, and remember him who wrote it. For the careless and rough handling of holy books is a sign of impiety. Be well, and may you live long" (codex 865, f. 297ʳ, 16th century).

Of great value are also the **short chronicles,** or brief accounts of events which were written by contemporary observers in the margins, or on the blank pages of the codices. They refer to important, historical events, natural catastrophies, or the history of the island and Monastery: "1647, 2nd of February: Here I wish to remind you of the great hunger, and how the price of bread rose to two astlania per

Ο ΑΓΙΟΣ ΓΡΙΓΟΡΙΟΣ Ο ΘΕΟΛΟΓΟΣ

Ο ΑΓΙΟΣ ΒΑΣΙΛΕΙΟΣ

Ο ΑΓΙΟΣ ΙΩΑΝΝΗΣ Ο ΧΡΥΣΟ

Ο ΑΓΙΟΣ ΝΙΚΟΛΑΟΣ

kilo, and 3 years have passed since the lawless nations began to wage war on Crete, that is, since 1645..." (Codex 623, 16th century, f 298). On the following page, in the same codex, we read: "In the year of our Lord 1646, Rethymnos was taken. And in the same year, on January the 5th, as dawn was breaking there were two tremendous earthquakes which made one think that the world was coming to an end. And every day the earth shook, for a period of two months. And in the above mentioned year, there was plague in Crete and it spread from one day to the other and mowed down Turks, Franks and Greeks alike".

The **old,** professional, **manuscript catalogue** of 1890, contains 890 works of which 855 are codices (292 on parchment and 563 on paper) and 35 liturgical scrolls, 35 on parchment and 2 on paper. Recent research has brought the number up to approx. 1000, of which 178 have been accurately dated. The manuscripts are classified by centuries as follows: 1,6th century; 2, 8th century; 9, 9th century; 39, 10th century; 77, 11th century; 86, 12th century; 61, 13th century; 64, 14th century; 86, 15th century; 89, 16th century; 93, 17th century; 216, 18th century; 35, 19th century. Almost all are written in Greek. There is one which is bilingual (413), three which are written in Latin (one of which is by Erasmus no 323), one in Hebrew (11th century) and two in Slavonic. As far as content is concerned, over 180 codices are liturgical in character (Gospels, Psalters, Breviaries, acts of Apostles, musicals); about 100 are Patristic Texts (St. John Chrysostomos, St. Basis, St. Gregory the Theologian, and others); some 50 deal with Canon Law and a further 50 with Lives of the Saints. Numerous codices contain philological works and Orations, some, the work of Byzantine and modern Greek authors, others treatises on asceticism, Bibles, etc. Only three codices contain classical texts: The Historical Library of Diodorus Siculus (Codex 50) dating from the 10th century; Euripides' Tragedies "Hecuba" and "Orestes" (Codex 433) dated 1442; and Sophocles' "Ajax" and the "Electra" (Codex 424) dating from the 15th century. In 1803, the traveller Clarke was responsible for removing from the Library a 9th century codex containing the Works of Plato, and other manuscripts which can be consulted today in the British Museum. Mention must also be made of some more recent manuscripts of classical texts (Lucian, Homer's Iliad, Isocrates) which date from the 17th and 18th centuries. (This classification of Codices according to subject and date is purely indicative some codices have mixed subjects and chronology, while the dating of some is still uncertain or approximative.)

The oldest codex in the Library dates from the 6th century (No 67) and contains **passages from the Gospel according to St. Mark:** (6,53; 7,4; 7,20; 8,32; 9,1; 10,43; 11,7; 12,19; 14,25; 15,23). It is composed of 33 very thin, porphyry pages in parchment. Pages from the same codex, namely 182, are to be found in the Leningrad Library; 2 in the Vienna Library; 4 in the British Museum; 6 in the Vatican; and one in the Athens Byzantine Museum. It has been copied by a competent scribe in large, round, silver letters. The text is arranged in two columns. The titles are placed on the upper margin and are composed of smaller, gold letters. Sacred names are also written in gold letters, f.e., IC (Jesus) XC (Christ) etc. The text is continuous, that is, there are no spaces between letters and periods, no chapter divisions, only one accent is used, and one punctuation mark the semicolon which is not always placed where and when needed. There are many spelling

26. St. John dictates to Prochoros, Illumination, codex 81 (p. 9).

mistakes, though not as many as one encounters in the older and more renowned manuscripts of mount Sinai and the Vatican.

The second oldest codex (No 171) dates from the beginning of the 8th century. It was copied by an excellent calligraphist. The text is the **Book of Job** and the script is in large, round letters placed in the centre of the page. Different versions of the text are given in small, angular letters between the lines of the text proper, and in the margins small, angular, capital letters (Unciales) are used for the hermeneutic analysis based on 19 ancient commentators. The codex is composed of 247 large pages in parchment. Few are missing from the beginning and the middle of the text. The codex contains 44 illuminations the themes of which are taken from the text itself. The artist was rather mediocre and the work betrays a remote influence of the Hellenistic tradition. Quite successful are his renderings of real or phantastical animals. On the contrary, the rendering of the human body is poor, though the figures present some interest from the sartorial point of view.

Codex No 33 is mentioned in the catalogue of 1200 "Great Book of the complete works of the Theologian". It is the work of competent, and relatively well educated scribes. It contains two books composed of **The Orations of Gregory the Theologian** and commentaries on the Orations written on 240 large pages in parchment of which 39 are missing. It was written in the year 941 at Reggio of Calabria, Italy, "by the hand of Nicholas the monk and his son Daniel, both Orthodox Christians..." as the note at the end confirms. Every page is divided in 3 columns of 50 lines, with scholia on the margins in small, angular letters. Every oration begins with multi-coloured, decorative interlacings and ornamental initials. Each new book, and the first 4 pages are richly decorated. Vivid colours, spiral and wavy designs and a perfect symmetry in the composition of the borders, betray a profound influence on the artist of mosaic pavements. His naturalism finds inspiration in the floral and animal designs of mosaic murals. These representations add variety to the geometricity of the borders. The human figure is rarely, and if so clumsily represented in the decorative patterns of the Initials.

The Patmian Library contains a representative, uninterrupted series of **illuminations** from the 9th to the 15th century. Most of these illuminations have been dated. The calligraphist monks came from different places and the techniques which they employed for manuscript illumination were the ones known in those days: full-page illuminations, inside or below the text, vignettes of different shapes and on different parts of the page, initials richly coloured and finely drawn. Durability and quality vary. Of particular interest are the full-page illuminations of the Four Gospels and the Initials on scrolls 1,22, and others. In a book of the Four Gospels (No. 80, 11th or 12th century) the four Evangelists are depicted in traditional poses: in meditation, while writing, or at their reading-desk. The vivid colours of these illuminations are wonderfully preserved. The background to the figures is composed of rich architectural detail, while the figures of the Evangelists are rendered in a most skilful way. All these factors make codex No 80 one of the most valuable possessions of the monastery (fig. 14). In codex 75 (12th century) we see again representations of the four Evangelists depicted in different poses within borders which decorate the upper third of one of the text's columns. The heads are emphasized and the facial expressions are very strong (fig. 17). Codex 274 (13th century) again figures representations of the four Evangelists combined on the same page

27. "Epigonation": (p. 57).

with narratives which take up the largest part of the upper section of the page (Birth and Baptism of Christ; Birth of St. John the Baptist (fig. 15) etc.). Finally, codex 81 (1345) is interesting for its beautiful binding, lovely first page vignettes opposite the Evangelists, finely drawn borders and skilful rendering of facial expressions (fig. 18). Illuminations, vignettes and decorative initials are to be found in codices: 22, 45, 72, 73, 74, 79, 83, 84, 87, 92, 97, 122, 134; vignettes and decorative initials in codices: 30, 40, 43, 44, 68, 69, 142 and on scrolls.

The Library contains two palimpsests of which codex No. 32 is one. The older script of church hymns was replaced in the 13th century by the text of a dictionary. Scraping off the old text in order to use again the parchment was a relatively widespread practice in medieval times mainly because the price of parchment was very high. Old bindings which have survived intact can be seen in codices 67, 81, 274, while the bindings of codices 74, 75, 79 and others, are partly destroyed.

28. "Epigonation": The Washing of the feet (p. 57).

The number of **printed books** which the Library possesses is about 3.000 volumes. The oldest printed book is an **Anthology of various epigrams by a group of ancient thinkers,** which was printed in Florence in 1494. Next comes the **Introduction to Grammar in four books, by Theodoros,** printed in Venice in 1495. The third oldest book is the **Argonautica** of Apollonius of Rhodes, printed in Florence in 1496. Altogether, there are eleven books surviving from the period before 1500. There are 45 16th century books, 7 of which are biblical texts and commentaries and 5 works of Aristotle. In the 17th century the number of books increases to appr. 130. These are mainly patristic works as well as Bibles and biblical commentaries. There are 223 books dating from the 18th century. We then note the appearance, for the first time, of books on physics and mathematics, political and church history, school books, poetry, history, as well as a number of treatises on apologetics and edification. The Patmian Library tries to keep up, as far as possible, with the great intellectual currents of the day. The largest collection dates from the 19th century and covers adequately many subjects: theology, history, education, physics, mathematics, byzantine and classical thought. Preferences in the field of classics are quite revealing: in Philosophy, there are 24 copies of Plato and 8 of Aristotle; in Oratory, 28 of Demosthenes and 14 of Isocrates; in Poetry, 42 of Homer and 29 of Euripides; in History, 34 of Xenophon and 25 of Thucydides; Plutarch surpasses them all: there are 56 copies of his works! Although the collection of printed books is not very rich, nonetheless it is of great interest because of the old, rare editions and the direct, or indirect information it provides concerning the intellectual interests reigning in the Monastery during each period.

Today, the Library, which has an exemplary organisation, is housed in rooms which have been specially equipped with air conditioning. The Photography Laboratory answers the needs of scholars from all over the world by providing slides, photographs and microfilms.

THE ARCHIVES

The Archives of the Monastery are, with the exception, perhaps, of analogous ones in the monasteries of Mount Athos, the only ones in the area of the Aegean presenting an almost continuous series of documents from the time of the foundation of the Monastery to the present (13.000 documents). Thanks to these documents, we can form a very clear picture of the Monastery's history concerning the expansion of its landed property from Asia Minor to the Ionian Islands and its relations with rulers and dignitaries through the years. The archives concerning political and economic history inform us not only about the Monastery's Land holdings in other places, whose number rendered it one of the greatest land proprietors of the Aegean, but also about Hellenism in general. Of particular interest on this subject are

29. Reliquary of the Blessed Christodoulos (p. 33).

data coming from the 16th century, for we lack information on public and private life during this century.

The documents connected with the Byzantine period (1073-1453) constitute one of the richest collections in the world. Though few in number (approx. 125 excluding multiple copies) these documents are an invaluable source of information on history and chancellery practices. They cover a period of five centuries: there are 30 belonging to the 11th century, 80 to the 12th and 13th centuries, 10 to the 15th and 16th centuries. They concern a wide geographical area (from Crete to Constantinople and from Eubea to Asia Minor), and provide us with information on more general topics and historical events. More especially, they widen our knowledge about the finances of the Monastery (income, tax exemptions, ownership of boats, settlers) and other activities. The documents are imperial, administrative, patriarchal, or private. Some of these documents are rare samples chancellery practices like the one of the officer "of the Kaniklion", the inventory of documents composed *circa* 1200, and the ratified collection of 10 official documents from 1100/15 which can be said, to be the longest surviving byzantine document: its length, at present, is 8.068 m. Some documents are of special importance for the history of the Monastery, for example, the Monastic Rule of the Blessed Christodoulos, his secret testament and his Codicil.

From the same period come the first Papal bulls in support of the Monastery (Pius II in 1461, Leo I in 1413) and several others issued by the grand masters of the Hospitalers in Rhodes, and the dukes and high officials in Venice.

All but a few documents refer to concessions made, to recognition of the privilege of autonomy enjoyed by the Monastery, to the purchase of new estates, the ratification of ownership for old ones, acquisition of settlers, exemption of ships from duties, donations, etc. The documents issued by the Superiors of the Monastery are of great interest not only because they enable us to form a picture of the Monastery's inner life, but also because of the style in which they are written and the vividness of the experiences recounted: time is cancelled and we feel as though the monks who penned them stand before us.

The Archives from the period of the Turkish occupation (1400-1912) include documents in Greek, Turkish (apprx. 1300), Roumanian (36), Latin (68), Russian, of which the oldest date from 1656-1705, and Georgian. The main body of the archives is composed of **Greek documents** dealing with the relations between the Monastery and the Patriarchate of Constantinople, under whose jurisdiction the Monastery lay, or with the neighbouring church dignitaries, and the Turkish admiral, since the Monastery lay under his administrative jurisdiction, or with his subordinates. The relations of the monastery with the island's lay community are also dealt with since the community enjoys now an independence in administration and finance. The documents relevant to monastic land property ("metochia") form a special unit, so do the ones dealing with the school of the Apocalypse. The **Turkish documents** are about 100 and for the most part decrees issued by the Sultan (firmans). Approximately 50 are decrees issued by the Captain Pashas, and a number are acts of contract (hotzetia). The **Latin documents** (68, 1296-1781), deal with the Monastery's relations with Venice (32), the Great Masters of Rhodes and, generally, with the Catholic powers, and refer to the privileges (mainly protection from piracy) granted to the Monastery by the Princes of the West (see p. 18) and the permissions of entrance to their countries for alms (see p. 18).

Also, permission to enter the estate of St. John the Stylite which the Monastery had in Crete, then under Venetian rule, from where another 360 documents and other acts were issued and preserved in the Archives. The **Roumanian documents,** with the exception of one, all refer to the help which the principalities along the Danube extended to the Monastery and the Patmian school, for the brightest, poor students. The greatest part of these documents is composed of acts of princes (22) by which Moldavia (1584) and Walachia (1670) renew certain subsidies which become regular and are granted yearly as of the beginning of the 18th century. The relations of the Monastery with these countries are positive and rewarding because of the deep sentiment of forming a united religious and spiritual community. The fame of the Monastery and of the school; the Greek descent of many rulers; the visits of Greek prelates to their courts, help to keep alive the old tradition of extending support to monasteries, and encourage the modern practice of giving political support to education in the orthodox countries which are under the Turkish yoke. The annual subsidies are complemented by extraordinary grants (for buildings, etc.) and precious gifts. The rulers ask in exchange the intercession of the monks for the Ruler, the members of his family and his kingdom. The smallest category of these documents refers to alms (see p. 18) which were collected by the Superior of the Monastery James in the years 1815-16 in the northeastern provinces of Moldavia (it is only from this area that the lists of donations have survived). One document refers to the dedication of a Roumanian Monastery as a holding ("metochi") to the Monastery of Patmos (1759).

There is a vast amount of material relevant to regional, general and diplomatic history, as well as on sigillography.

Today, the temporary exhibit contains many documents worthy of attention: codices on parchment, dating from early periods, with beautiful illuminations and bindings; codices in paper when the use of paper was beginning to spread (12th century), important documents and, finally, some old editions of books (before 1500) preserved in the Library (see p. 50).

THE TREASURY

The Monastery's treasury is rich in the possession of priceless objects which fall under four categories: sacred relics, fragments of the Holy Cross (p. 36); icons; silverwork connected with ritual needs; vestments. The oldest possessions were obtained for the Monastery by the Founder. The oldest surviving catalogue was composed by the Superior Arsenios (1200). Documents which are to be found in the archives, oral tradition and inscriptions allow us to reconstruct satisfactorily the history of the Treasury. The greatest part of these sacred object belong to the period 1600-1800; very few belong to the byzantine period. One of the main reasons is the turbulent history of the Monastery and of the island: "... golden and silver treasures do not seek to find in the Superior's cell because thou shalt not find... I have not collected riches while I have been the Superior, for my only concern was trying to meet the basic needs of the Monastery and ensuring its protection from the pirates..." (Testament of the Superior Germanos, 1272). The objects were mainly offerings usually given by clerics. These donors were church dignitaries the most important of

30. Gospel binding: the Apocalypse (p. 57). →

which were Patmiot prelates active in other lands, for example the Patriarch of Constantinople Neophytos 6th, the Metropolitans: of Carpathos Neophytos Grymanis, of Didimotychon Michael, of Sebasteia Daniel, of Sardis Nectarios, the hieromonk James Anastasios and others who had at one time been connected with the Monastery, or who had come to finish their days there, like the bishops: of Laodicea Nicephoros (a Cretan) of Smyrna Methodios, of Demetsana and Argyrocastron Nicodemos (1727), of Didimotichon Gregory (from Cos). Valuable offerings were also given by the rulers of the Danube principalities, for example Michael Constantine Soutzos, and some of the Russian kings, Peter the Great and Catherine II.

The inscriptions we find on these objects reveal the names, titles and birthplace of the donors, some even reveal aspects of their personality, or inform us about the artistic centres of the period, the workshops where these sacred objects were produced: Bucarest, Jena, Nizni-Nogvorod, Trapezounda, Constantinople, Mount Athos, Trieste, Smyrna, Patmos.

A letter written by the Patmiots to Patriarch Samuel (1763-68) reveals their attitude towards the Monastery and its relics: "Because, we christians who dwell on this arid, barren island have nothing else to make us feel proud and honoured [...] but this holy, royal Monastery [...] and find support in it and are raised by it, and seeing there the old sacred offerings and relics of our ancestors, not only do our souls overflow with joy, but we feel as if those who gave the offerings are present and alive, gazing upon them with pleasure, and even so, willingly and devoutly each one of us offers new ones and dedicates whatever he wishes (1763-68).

As yet, no systematic research and publication on the relics has appeared.

The Monastery possesses over 200 **icons** dating from various periods. Of these, the most valuable are the byzantine ones. A very rare specimen of this period is the small mosaic icon of St. Nicholas (0.217x0.185) dating from the 11th century. The Saint is depicted in an upright position giving his blessing (see fig. 19). On his right stands Christ offering him the Gospel, while on his left stands the Virgin presenting him with an "omophorion". This is a representation of the prophetic dream which made known to the Saint his future rise to the throne of an archbishop. The silver encasing of the frame is ornamented with medallions depicting the preparation of the Throne, two angels and four warrior saints (13th/14th century).

A true masterpiece is the icon representing the warrior saint Theodoros of Tyros dating from the 12th of 13th century (see fig. 22). To the same period belongs the imposing icon representing St. James (fig. 20). Icons dating from the 15th century include: the Assumption of the Blessed Virgin (fig. 23), two icons of St. Nicholas, the purification of the Virgin (fig. 24) and Christ enthroned. To the 16th century belong an icon of Christ enthroned, the Virgin, painted by the great painter Andreas Ritzos, the 40 Martyrs, the Annunciation, the round icon of the Kiss of the Apostles Peter and Paul, and the triptych representing the twelve major feasts of the Orthodox Church, painted by the well-known artist George Clotzas. This icon deserves attention because of its excellent miniature technique, the complexity of its composition and its vivid colouring. Of interest are, also, that of St. John the Divine (see fig. 2), and two "panagiaria". Icons dating from the 17th century are numerous: St. George, The Nativity, The Immaculate Virgin, (in the chapel of the Founder).

The **liturgical vestments** number over 600 and belong mainly to the

17th and 18th centuries. They are made of precious cloth and are richly embroidered with gold, silver and silk thread representing saints and scenes from the life of Christ or of the Virgin. These representations in embroidery are often works of great art revealing the talent and sensitivity of the anonymous artist in the delicate use of colour, the expertise in composition and design and the close relation in the iconography and style with the great art of the Byzantine period. These sacred embroideries include series of vestments which are rare and priceless for Orthodoxy. They cover a period of three centuries (15th-18th) and the first and most valuable collection consists of "epitrachilia" which are, indeed, masterpieces of portraiture (see fig. 25) and of decorative design. Another important series are the "epigonatia" dating from the 15th century. The oldest depicts the Sleeping Christ (see fig. 27) and St. Luke (modelled after a miniature) with portraits of saints around. To the 16th and 17th centuries belong those of the Last Supper, the Washing of the Feet (see fig. 28) and the Transfiguration. The facial expression, the use of colour and the sense of perspective render these embroideries true works of art. To the 18th century belong two "epigonatia" representing the Trinity (embroidered by the famous embroideress Eusebia) and the Entombment. These are excellent pieses of work and, what is of interest, free from western influences which are very pronounced in the "epigonation" of the Apocalypse. There are a few but precious "epitaphioi" especially two large ones dating from the 15th century. Another important though small collection is that of "omophoria". It is interesting to compare the earlier (15th century) with the latter ones (18th century) and follow the development of the art of embroidery from byzantine to post-byzantine times. The iconography presents great similarities but the techniques have radically changed. Other categories of embroidered work include maniples, covers, mitres, screens, some of which are on exhibition.

The collection of **silverwork** includes today over 300 pieces. These objects are made of silver or are gilted and date mostly from the 17th and 18th centuries. They are decorated with engravings, filligree and enamel work and bear inscriptions relating to the craftsman or the owner. There are very few objects made of gold, usually crosses and amulets which also bear precious stones. Many of these are of a more recent date and are used in the daily liturgy or on feast days. The Treasury contains a rich collection of silver chandeliers and lamps manufactured in distant workshops. Of interest is the collection of staffs, one of the most precious of which is the staff of the archbishop Dionysios IV (1677) presented to the Monastery by the Patmiot Patriarch of Constantinople Neophytos VI (fig. 31). The collection includes pastoral crosses, amulets, crosses for blessing, for sanctification, etc., as well as chalices (many come from the West) (fig. 32). Of special interest are the precious amulets, crosses and golden medals presented to the Monastery by Peter the Great and Catherine II of Russia. There are also censers, candlesticks, trays, gilt icons and reliquaries, ripidia and Gospels in silver binding (1697, 1787, fig. 30).

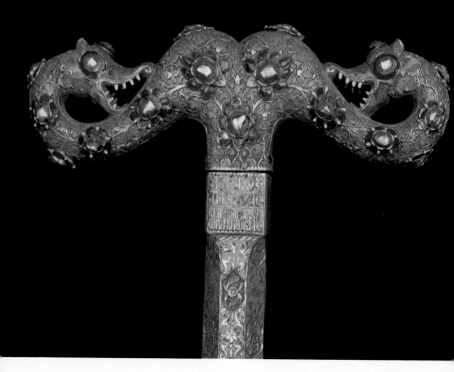

31. *Upper part of a Bishop's staff (p. 57).*

BIBLIOGRAPHY

GENERAL: **1.** Collected Bibliography to 1960 in *Δωδεκανησιακὴ Βιβλιογραφία* by N. Μαυρῆς, Α΄-Γ΄, Athens (1964-1974) (as yet the third volume not in circulation), for every main subject, chapters on Patmos. **2.** Παπαδόπουλος, Στ. ᾿Α., *Πάτμος, ὁδηγὸς τοῦ ἐπισκέπτη,* Athens, 1967. Published by: Monastery of St. John the Theologian. **3.** Μαραβᾶ-Χατζηνικολάου, ῎Αννα, *Πάτμος,* Athens, 1957. Publ.: French Institute (Bibliography and illustrations. New edition, 1971, condensed with more illustrations and published by "Astir"). **4.** Geil, W.E., *The isle that is called Patmos,* London, 1905. **5.** Article in *Real Encycl.* vol. XVIII, 4, col. 2174-2191. Extensive bibliography. **6.** Gerola, G., "I monumenti mediaevali delle tredici Sporadi", *Ann. Scuola Arch. Atene* 2 (1915), 84-97 (for the Monastery).

HISTORY: For the History of the maritime isle of the Aegean and the Mediterranean in general and from a geographical-anthropological point of view see: **7.** Braudel, F., *La Méditerranée et le monde méditerranéen à l'époque de Philippe II,* I, Paris, 1966, 94-152. For ancient times see 5, and in addition: **8.** Pace, B., "Ricordi classici dell'isola di Patmos", *Ann. Scuola Arch. Atene* 1(1914), 370-372. **9.** Manganaro, G., "Le iscrizioni delle isole Milesie", *Ann. Scuola Arch.*

Atene 41-42 (1963-1964), 293-349. **10.** Saffrey, H.B., "Relire l'Apocalypse à Patmos", *Revue Biblique* 82 (1975), 385-417. For the Byzantine Period: **11.** Βρανούση, "Ερα Λ., *Τὰ ἁγιολογικὰ κείμενα τοῦ Ὁσίου Χριστοδούλου, φιλολογικὴ παράδοσις καὶ ἱστορικαὶ μαρτυρίαι,* Athens, 1960 (extensive bibliography). **12.** Miklosich, Fr. - Müller, Ios., *Acta et Diplomata graeca medii aevi,* I - VI, Vienna, 1890 (texts of major documents from Archives). **13.** Lavagnini, B., "I Normanni di Sicilia a Cipro e a Patmo (1186), *Bizantino-Sicula II (=Miscellanea G. Rossi Taibbi),* Palermo, 1974, 321-344. **14.** Vranoussi, Era, "A propos des opérations des Normands dans la mer Égée et à Chypre après la prise de Thessalonique (1185-1186)", *Βυζαντινὰ* 8 (1976), 205-211. For period of Turkish occupation: the 170 Travellers who refer to Patmos: see in 1, vol. Β΄, 117-252 also under «Πάτμος» in 6.: 251. The main informations provided by them is included in the chapter on the island's history in the Present guide and in: **15.** Μαλανδράκης, Μ., «Νησιωτικὰ Χρονικὰ» (part I published in 10th and 11th volumes of *Ἑλληνικά·* part II in book form Athens, 1940. **16.** Μαλανδράκης, Μ., *Ἡ Πατμιὰς Σχολή,* Athens 1911 (see also 1, vol. Α΄, 257-259). **17.** Hofmann, G., "Patmos und Rom", *Orientalia Cristiana,* XI-2 (1928), 1-107. **18.** Κρητικὸς, Π., «Πατμιακὰ τοπωνύμια», *Δωδεκανησιακὸν Ἀρχεῖον* 1 (1956), 57-110· 2 (1956), 102-157· 4 (1959-60), 33-94 and articles by same in *Δωδεκαν. Ἐπιθεώρηση).* **19.** Παπαδόπουλος, Στ. Ἀ., Ἐπιγραφές Ἰ. Μονῆς Ἰωάννου Θεολόγου, Athens, 1966, in *Ἐπιγραφὲς τῆς Πάτμου.* Publ. by Dept. of Antiquities, Bulletin of Archeology 9. **20.** Ζαχαριάδου, Ἐλισάβετ, «Συμβολὴ στὴν ἱστορία τοῦ νοτιοανατολικοῦ Αἰγαίου», *Σύμμεικτα* 1 (Athens 1966), 184-232. Publ. by Centre for Byzantine Studies. On the Metochia. **21.** Νυσταζοπούλου, Μαρία, «Τέσσερα ἄγνωστα ρωσικὰ ἔγγραφα ὑπὲρ τῆς ἐν Μήλῳ μονῆς τῆς Θεοτόκου (1656-1705)». *Σύμμεικτα* 1 (1966), 231-257. **22.** Βρανούση, "Ερα, "Ενα μετόχι τῆς Μονῆς Πάτμου στὴ Ζάκυνθο», *Πρακτικὰ Γ΄ Πανιονίου Συνεδρίου,* (Athens, 1967), 35-46. **23.** Ζερλέντης, Π., «Ἱστορικὰ σημειώματα ἐκ τοῦ Βραβείου τοῦ ἐν Πάτμῳ Μοναστηρίου Ἁγ. Ἰωάννου τοῦ Θεολόγου» in *Ἱστορικαὶ ἔρευναι περὶ τῆς ἐκκλησίας τῶν νήσων ...,* Hermoupolis, 1913-22, 157-215 καὶ 301-306. For the portrait, see 1, vol. Α΄, 113-116. For surviving inscriptions 1773, see: **24.** Σακκελίων, Ἰ., «Ἔγγραφα Ἱστορικά», *Πανδώρα* 10, 126-132, for that of 1827, see 2, p. 7.

32. Cross and chalices (p. 57).

FOR THE MONASTERY: for general information see: 1 vol. A΄, 127-134. ARCHITECTURE - PAINTING. **25.** 'Ορλάνδος, 'Αν. Κ., *Ή ἀρχιτεκτονικὴ καὶ αἱ βυζαντιναὶ τοιχογραφίαι τῆς Μονῆς Θεολόγου Πάτμου*, Athens, 1970. Publ. by The Athens Academy (covers all previous Bibliography). **26.** Φατούρου, Κάντω Χ., *Ή ἐκκλησία τῶν Ἁγίων 'Αποστόλων, ὡς δεῖγμα χαρακτηριστικῆς πατμιακῆς τεχνοτροπίας*. Athens, Publ. Dept. of Antiquities, Bulletin of Archeology 2. **27.** Φατούρου, Κάντω Χ., Οἰκοδομικὲς ἐπιγραφὲς τοῦ μοναστηριοῦ τοῦ Ἁγ. 'Ιωάννου Θεολόγου στὴν Πάτμο, Athens, 1966, in *'Επιγραφὲς τῆς Πάτμου*, publ. Dept. of Antiquities, Bulletin of Archeology, 9.
FOR THE LIBRARY: **28.** Σακκελίων, 'Ι., *Πατμιακὴ Βιβλιοθήκη*, Athens, 1890. **29.** Καλλίμαχος, Δ., «Πατμιακῆς Βιβλιοθήκης: Συμπλήρωμα», *Ἐκκλησιαστ. Φάρος* 10-17 (1912-1918). **30.** Κομίνης, 'Αθ., «Σακκελίωνος Παραλειπόμενα», *Σύμμεικτα* 1 (1966), 35-76. (See also 1, vol. A΄, 17-22). **31.** Diehl, Ch., "Le trésor et la bibliothèque de Patmos au commencement du 13ᵉ s.", *Byz. Zeitschrift* 1 (1892), 488-525. **32.** Βρανούση, "Ερα, «'Ο καθηγούμενος τῆς Μονῆς Πάτμου 'Ιωσὴφ 'Ιασίτης καὶ ἡ ἀρχαιότερη ἀναγραφὴ χειρογράφων τῆς Μονῆς», *Δελτίον Χριστ. 'Αρχαιολ. 'Εταιρείας* Δ΄, 4 (1964), 345-352, pl. 73. **33.** Βρανούση, "Ερα, «Σάββας, καθηγούμενος τῆς Μονῆς Πάτμου», *Ἑλληνικὰ* 19 (1966), 216-225. **34.** Κομίνης, 'Αθ., «'Ο νέος κατάλογος τῶν χειρογράφων τῆς ἐν Πάτμω ἱερᾶς μονῆς 'Ιωάννου τοῦ Θεολόγου (Μέθοδος καὶ προβλήματα)», *Σύμμεικτα* 1 (1966), 17-34. **35.** Κομίνης, 'Αθ., *Πίνακες χρονολογημένων πατμιακῶν κωδίκων*, Athens, 1967. Komines, Ath., *Facsimiles of dated Patmian Codices*, Athens, 1970. **36.** Κομίνης, 'Αθ., «Πατμιακά, ἡ μαρτυρία δύο βιβλιογραφικῶν προσθηκῶν», *'Ερανιστὴς* 5, fasc. 30 (1967), 194-200. **37.** Darrouzès, J., "Un recueil épistolaire byzantin. Le manuscrit de Patmos 706", *Revue des Études Byzantines* 14 (1956), 87-121. **38.** Épistoliers Byzantins du Xe siècle, édités par J. Darrouzès. Institut Français d'Études byzantines, Paris, 1960.
FOR THE TREASURY: **39.** Jacopi, G., "Le Miniature dei codici di Patmo, cimeli del ricamo, della pittura e della toreutica nel tresoro del Monastero di Patmos", *Clara Rodos* 6-7, part III (1932-33). **40.** Μαραβᾶ-Χατζηνικολάου, "Αννα, «'Η ψηφιδωτὴ εἰκόνα τῆς Πάτμου», *Δελτίον Χριστ. 'Αρχαιολ. 'Εταιρείας* Δ΄, 1 (1959), 127-34. **41.** Παπαδόπουλος, Στ. 'Α., «Νεοφύτου τοῦ ΣΤ΄, πατριάρχου Κωνσταντινουπόλεως, ἔγγραφα καὶ ἀφιερώματα πρὸς τὴν 'Ι. Μονὴν 'Ιωάννου Θεολόγου Πάτμου», *Χαριστήριον εἰς Α.Κ. 'Ορλάνδον*, IV, Athens 1967, 220-246, πίν. LXXVII-LXXXVIII. See also no **14.** For illustrations see: **42.** *'Η Βυζαντινὴ Τέχνη, τέχνη εὐρωπαϊκή*, Guide of 9th Exhibition Council of Europe, Athens, 1964.
ARCHIVES: **43.** Dölger, F., "Die Kaiserurkunden des Johannes Theologos Kloster auf Patmos", *Byz. Zeitschrift* 28 (1928), 332-371. **44.** Βρανούση, "Ερα, «'Ανέκδοτος Κατάλογος ἐγγράφων τῆς ἐν Πάτμω Μονῆς (ΙΒ΄-ΙΓ΄ αἰ.)», *Σύμμεικτα* 1 (1966), 137-162. **45.** Vranoussi, Era, "Contribution à l'étude de la paléographie diplomatique: les actes de Patmos", *Colloques Internationaux du C.N.R.S.* no 559. La paléographie grecque et byzantine, Paris, 1974 (Under print). **46.** *Τὰ βυζαντινὰ Ἔγγραφα τῆς Μονῆς Πάτμου*, Ι: *"Εγγραφα αὐτοκρατορικά*, ed. "Ερα Λ. Βραούση. Publ.: Centre for Byzantine Studies, Athens (Under print). **47.** Νυσταζοπούλου-Πελεκίδου, Μαρία - Mircea, I.- R., «Τὰ ρουμανικὰ ἔγγραφα τοῦ ἀρχείου τῆς ἐν Πάτμω Μονῆς», *Σύμμεικτα* 2 (1970), 255-320. **48.** Μαλτέζου, Χρύσα, «Τὰ λατινικὰ ἔγγραφα τοῦ Πατμιακοῦ ἀρχείου», *Σύμμεικτα* 2 (1970), 349-378. See also fasc. 21. **49.** Παναγιωτόπουλος,